Editor

Lorin Klistoff, M.A.

Editor in Chief

Karen J. Goldfluss, M.S. Ed.

Cover Artist

Brenda DiAntonis

Illustrator

Teacher Created Resources Staff

Art Coordinator

Renée Christine Yates

Imaging

Leonard P. Swierski

Publisher

Mary D. Smith, M.S. Ed.

TCR 2435

TARGETING GRAMMAR 4-5

Lessons, practice & MORE!

Includes Standards & Benchmarks

Interactive games & literacy center activities

Ideas for getting students actively involved

Word banks & other handy references

Teacher Created Resources

Author

Teacher Created Resources

The classroom teacher may reproduce copies of materials in this book for classroom use only. Reproduction of any part for an entire school or school system is strictly prohibited. No part of this publication may be transmitted, stored, or recorded in any form without written permission from the publisher.

Teacher Created Resources, Inc.

6421 Industry Way

Westminster, CA 92683

www.teachercreated.com

ISBN: 978-1-4206-2435-9

© 2009 Teacher Created Resources, Inc.

Made in U.S.A.

Teacher Created Resources

Section 1 CONTENTS

NOUNS 17

ADJECTIVES 35

PRONOUNS 47

VERBS. 57

Section 2 CONTENTS

GAMES & ACTIVITIES. 121

Like art and music, language can rise to the highest form of expression. Like art, it has composition, balance, and color. Like music it has rhythm, harmony, and fluidness. And like all art, it can touch the heart and inspire the soul. We speak and our words fade away on a breath. Yet, what impressions we can leave behind!

In a busy modern world, language, in all its technical and creative brilliance, is often outshone by the very stimulating audio-visual world of multimedia. Many of our children are stepping into a world of virtual reality, which only requires their passive acquiescence. As teachers in this modern world, we have to equip our young people with the skills they need to communicate easily and successfully. It is not enough to get by with an oral vernacular and text message shorthand. Employers require workers who can speak eloquently and confidently. They need workers who can write in succinct and precise ways using correct grammar and spelling. Without the facility of using language to express themselves orally and in the written form, people can become excluded and powerless in many areas of business and society.

For too long, the teaching of grammar has been discounted as being outdated and irrelevant. Yet grammar is at the heart and soul of language. As teachers, we need to help our young people develop the skills they need to express themselves creatively and meaningfully; to be able to critically evaluate the myriad texts that surround them every day. This book is intended for use by teachers to help their students build a strong and solid foundation for language use. It draws on a traditional model relevant to a modern world. We cannot be critical of what we see, hear, and read if we don't know how the creators of text manipulate words and language through their grammatical choices. As teachers we need to instruct our students in these underlying structures and patterns and ways of making meaning. Part of using text "in context" is to understand how the text itself is created. Grammar does and will continue to play a central role in the composition of our language, both oral and written.

Language has not been "created" for our use. We use it to create our reality, our lives, and our relationships. Without it, we are powerless.

This book presents detailed knowledge of correct English grammar and its application in spoken and written language, relevant to this level of schooling. Both teacher and students can examine and explore language, leading to deeper understandings and improved technique.

HOW TO USE THIS BOOK

Section 1 of this book is divided into the following subsections:

1. Nouns   5. Adverbs
2. Adjectives   6. Prefixes
3. Pronouns   7. Prepositions and Phrases
4. Verbs   8. Sentences

Each subsection contains the following:

A Note to the Teacher Knowledge of the topic is stripped to its bare bones. This information serves as the basis for the explicit teaching to follow. For some, this will be a refresher course. For others, it may be a first introduction to grammar in all its depth and beauty.

Introducing Ideas Included in the notes are suggestions for ways of introducing specific grammar concept to students. The ideas begun here are developed in the student pages that follow.

Exploring Ideas This page offers ideas for getting students actively involved in an exploration of the area of study to build understanding.

Student Pages The student pages have been designed for students to examine and explore the technical aspects of grammar and its practical application. Scaffolds are in place to support learning with each grammar concept written at the top of each student page. Teachers need to explicitly teach these concepts before presenting the student page to students.

Assessment Assessment items have marks allocated. The marking system allows the teacher to evaluate, analyze, and pinpoint areas of individual and class need. Reproducible marking grids for each section have been provided on the following pages to assist with monitoring individual students and/or whole class progress.

Section 2 of this book includes the following:

Games Games are ready-to-use and materials are clearly listed. Directions and suggestions follow for use with small groups of students. Games are an enjoyable way of reinforcing the language that students need to successfully use and understand grammar. Group games can help to reinforce students' understanding of grammar and, in many cases, the spelling closely associated with its use.

Grammar Task Cards The task cards have been designed especially for practicing grammatical concepts and knowledge. Like any other endeavor, we need exposure, focused attention, trial and error, application, and technical know-how. Above all, we need to practice what we think we know. Task cards are for individual use. They may be used by all students within a literacy center or by any individual student who requires further practice.

Word Banks A range of practical reference materials designed to save teacher's time.

Answer Key There is an answer key located at the end of the book for the student pages, games, and task cards.

Nouns
pages 33 – 34

Student Names

Maximum points	5	10	4	6	5	5	5	5	5	50
	Check 1	Check 2	Check 3	Check 4	Check 5	Check 6	Check 7	Check 8	Check 9	TOTAL
	identify nouns	recognize different noun types	identify noun types	build compound nouns	understand plural noun forms	identify noun-forming suffixes	identify noun phrases	use apostrophes to show possession	identify nouns in own writing	

ASSESSMENT RECORDS

Adjectives
pages 45 – 46

Maximum points	5	12	10	8	5	5	5	50
Student Names	Check 1 recognize adjective/ noun relationship	Check 2 understand adjective/ noun relationship	Check 3 identify adjectives	Check 4 understand the role of antonyms	Check 5 understand similes	Check 6 identify adjective- forming suffixes	Check 7 apply adjectives of degree	TOTAL

Pronouns
pages 55 – 56

Maximum points	5	10	12	8	5	10	50
	Check 1	Check 2	Check 3	Check 4	Check 5	Check 6	TOTAL
Student Names	recognize pronouns	identify pronouns	use pronouns correctly	understand pronoun/noun relationship	choose pronouns appropriately	apply pronoun/noun relationship	

Verbs
pages 75 – 76

Maximum points	10	10	10	5	5	5	5	50
	Check 1	Check 2	Check 3	Check 4	Check 5	Check 6	Check 7	TOTAL
Student Names	identify verbs/verb groups	identify verb tense	apply knowledge of homographs	choose appropriate "saying" verbs	apply knowledge of contractions	understand subject/verb agreement	correctly use present and past participle	

10

©*Teacher Created Resources, Inc.*

Adverbs
pages 85 – 86

Student Names	Maximum points 6 Check 1 understand the function of adverbs	10 Check 2 identify adverbs	8 Check 3 use "ly" to form adverbs	4 Check 4 use interrogative adverbs	6 Check 5 understand adverb/ verb relationship	6 Check 6 understand the role of antonyms	5 Check 7 discriminate between adjective and adverb	5 Check 8 choose adverbs appropriately	50 TOTAL

Prepositions & Phrases
pages 96 – 98

Student Names

Maximum points	10	6	4	5	5	5	5	5	5	50
	Check 1	Check 2	Check 3	Check 4	Check 5	Check 6	Check 7	Check 8	Check 9	TOTAL
	identify phrases	understand how prepositions position "things"	understand how phrases add meaning to sentences	understand function of adverbial phrases	recognize adjectival phrase/noun relationship	choose phrases appropriate to meaning	understand the function of adverbial phrases	apply knowledge of prepositions	discriminate between adjectival and adverbial phrases	

12 ©Teacher Created Resources, Inc.

Sentences
pages 118 – 120

Maximum points	5	5	5	5	5	5	5	3	3	2	7	50
	Check 1	Check 2	Check 3	Check 4	Check 5	Check 6	Check 7	Check 8	Check 9	Check 10	Check 11	TOTAL
Student Names	identify sentences as a unit	recognize statements as facts or opinions	compose questions	recognize the sentence pattern of commands	identify subject of sentences	use conjunctions to form compound sentences	identify principal and subordinate clauses	understand the function of subordinate clauses	correctly use relative pronouns	punctuate dialogue	punctuate a paragraph	

ASSESSMENT RECORDS

Summary

Student Names	NOUNS	ADJECTIVES	PRONOUNS	VERBS	ADVERBS	PREPOSITIONS AND PHRASES	SENTENCES	TOTAL
Maximum points	50	50	50	50	50	50	50	350

Focus	Wordworks pages 123–129	Shuffle 'n' Sort pages 130–152	Fact Finders pages 153–184	TASK CARDS pages 185–198
Adjectival phrases	✓			✓
Adjectives	✓	✓		✓
Adverbial phrases	✓			✓
Adverbs	✓			✓
Antonyms	✓		✓	✓
Collective nouns	✓			✓
Compound sentences				✓
Compound words	✓		✓	✓
Contractions	✓			✓
Definitions	✓			
Dictionary use	✓	✓	✓	✓
Exclamations				✓
Fact or opinion				✓
Gender	✓			
Homographs	✓			
Homophones			✓	
Noun phrases				✓
Nouns	✓			✓
Phrases	✓			✓
Plurals	✓			
Possessive nouns	✓			✓
Prepositions				✓
Pronouns	✓			✓
Proper nouns				✓
Punctuation				✓
Research skills			✓	
Sentences			✓	✓
Statements			✓	✓
Subject/predicate				✓
Subjects	✓			
Suffixes				✓
Tense	✓	✓		✓
Verbal adjectives	✓			✓
Verbs	✓	✓		✓
Verbs—"doing"	✓	✓		✓
Verbs—"saying"	✓	✓		✓
Vocabulary skills		✓		
Words in context			✓	✓

STANDARDS

The lessons and activities in this book meet the following standards and benchmarks, which are used with permission from McREL. (Copyright 2009 McREL. Mid-continent Research for Education and Learning, 4601 DTC Boulevard, Suite 500 Denver, CO 80237 Telephone: 303-337-0990 Website: www.mcrel.org/standards-benchmarks)

Standard 1: Uses the general skills and strategies of the writing process

- Editing and Publishing: Uses strategies to edit and publish written work (e.g., edits for grammar, punctuation, capitalization, and spelling at a developmentally appropriate level; uses reference materials; considers page format [paragraphs, margins, indentations, titles]; selects presentation format according to purpose; incorporates photos, illustrations, charts, and graphs; uses available technology to compose and publish work)

Standard 2: Uses the stylistic and rhetorical aspects of writing

- Uses descriptive language that clarifies and enhances ideas (e.g., common figures of speech, sensory details)

- Uses paragraph form in writing (e.g., indents the first word of a paragraph, uses topic sentences, recognizes a paragraph as a group of sentences about one main idea, uses an introductory and concluding paragraph, writes several related paragraphs)

- Uses a variety of sentence structures in writing (e.g., expands basic sentence patterns, uses exclamatory and imperative sentences)

Standard 3: Uses grammatical and mechanical conventions in written compositions

- Uses pronouns in written compositions (e.g., substitutes pronouns for nouns, uses pronoun agreement)

- Uses nouns in written compositions (e.g., uses plural and singular naming words, forms regular and irregular plurals of nouns, uses common and proper nouns, uses nouns as subjects)

- Uses verbs in written compositions (e.g., uses a wide variety of action verbs, past and present verb tenses, simple tenses, forms of regular verbs, verbs that agree with the subject)

- Uses adjectives in written compositions (e.g., indefinite, numerical, predicate adjectives)

- Uses adverbs in written compositions (e.g., to make comparisons)

- Uses coordinating conjunctions in written compositions (e.g., links ideas to connecting words)

- Uses conventions of spelling in written compositions (e.g., spells high frequency, commonly misspelled words from appropriate grade-level list; uses a dictionary and other resources to spell words; uses initial consonant substitution to spell related words; uses vowel combinations for correct spelling; uses contractions, compounds, roots, suffixes, prefixes, and syllable constructions to spell words)

- Uses conventions of capitalization in written compositions (e.g., titles of people; proper nouns [names of towns, cities, counties, and states; days of the week; months of the year; names of streets, names of countries; holidays]; first word of direct quotations; heading salutation, and closing of a letter)

- Uses conventions of punctuation in written compositions (e.g., uses periods after imperative sentences and in initials, abbreviations, and titles before names; uses commas in dates and addresses and after greeting and closings in a letter; uses apostrophes in contractions and possessive nouns; uses quotation marks around titles and with direct quotations; uses a colon between hour and minutes)

NOUNS

Nouns are the words that name the people, places, animals, and things in sentences.

A Note to the Teacher

A sentence is a group of words communicating a complete thought. Look at the examples below.

e.g., Red dust covered the town.

e.g., It leaked through doors and windows.

e.g., Soon it lay thick on tables and chairs.

We speak, and especially write, in sentences. A sentence is made up of a string of words, with each word having a particular job to do. Some words only have one job to do (e.g., *and, the, a, but*).

Others have different jobs in different sentences (e.g., Red *dust* covered the town. She will *dust* the tables and chairs.).

Some words, such as pronouns, also link ideas across sentences. Because they refer backwards and forwards to people and things, they tie ideas together and give text fluency and cohesion. A deep understanding of how words work enables speakers and writers to use language to communicate easily and successfully.

Carl went to the *shop* to buy
person   place
bones for his *dog.*
things   animal

Different nouns have different jobs to do.

Common nouns name the everyday things around us.

e.g., cup, horse, tree, arm, cheese, book, parrot, basket, clock, pie, pencil, car, rabbit, bridge, computer, soup

Proper nouns give people, places, objects, and events their given or special names.

They are easily recognized because they always begin with a capital letter.

e.g., Jane, Mars, Olympic Games, New York City, Grand Canyon, Sunday, Christmas, April, Swan River, India

Compound nouns are made by joining two words together.

e.g., snowflake, heartbeat, tablecloth, sandcastle, butterscotch, basketball

Possessive nouns show ownership. An apostrophe is always used.

e.g., Jack's horse, children's shoes, the teacher's book, Dad's beard, the cats' whiskers, six hens' eggs

Collective nouns are names given to groups of person or things.

e.g., flock (of birds), herd (of cows), crowd (of people), mob (of kangaroos), swarm (of bees)

Verbal nouns are present participles used as nouns.

e.g., Skiing is a winter sport. Let's go bowling. Skating on thin ice is dangerous. Seeing is believing.

Nouns may be singular or plural.

Singular nouns name one thing.

e.g., box, train, football, flower, match, rose

Plural nouns name more than one thing.

e.g., boxes, trains, footballs, flowers, matches, roses

Most plural nouns are formed by adding "s" or "es" to the singular noun.

Some plural nouns are formed by changing the vowels or adding "en."

e.g., foot—feet; man—men; child—children

Some nouns are both singular and plural.

e.g., sheep, fish, deer

Some nouns are only plural.

e.g., pants, scissors, cutlery

A **noun phrase** is a group of words built around a noun.

e.g., a tiny, black <u>spider</u>; a squat, brown <u>teapot</u>; one chocolate and almond <u>cake</u>; long-awaited <u>news</u>; my straw <u>hat</u>

These noun groups name the participants in the text.

e.g., <u>The three inexperienced schoolboys</u> became lost in the rain forest. <u>Many local people</u> joined in the search for them. They found <u>the cold, hungry, and frightened boys</u> sixteen hours later.

Articles

The articles *a*, *an*, and *the* are often used to introduce nouns groups. *A* and *an* are **indefinite articles** because they do not point to a particular thing. *An* is used before a word beginning with a vowel, or an unsounded "h."

e.g., a boy, a dog, a racing car, an egg, an ant, an old man, an opera, an hour

The is a **definite article** because it points to a known or particular thing.

e.g., the sun, the moon, the boy by the door, the house on the hill, the last page

Noun-forming suffixes

A *suffix* (word ending) changes the way a word is used in a sentence. Some suffixes added to words form nouns.

e.g., kind<u>ness</u>, judg<u>ment</u>, just<u>ice</u>, inten<u>tion</u>, danc<u>er</u>, violin<u>ist</u>, deliver<u>ance</u>, parent<u>hood</u>

Ideas for Introducing Nouns

- Ask some students to state their names and list them on the board.

- Ask them to name objects around them in the room and list these on the board.

- Talk about names and introduce the word *nouns*. These are the words that name all the things we can see, touch, feel, hear, and smell. Ask the students to use their senses (one at a time) to help you list some nouns on the board.

- Give the students some junk mail and ask them to give you some more nouns to list on the board.

- Write this sentence on the board:

> *Carl went to the store to buy bones for his dog.*

Discuss the nouns and what they name.

- Write other sentences to use as examples of how nouns name people and things in text.

- Let the students find and list some nouns in a book they are reading.

- Pin up a large picture and ask the students to name the people and/or objects in the picture.

- Invite the students to work in pairs to label as many nouns as they can on a picture from a magazine. These could be displayed for all to share.

- Start a wall chart headed "Nouns." This could be divided into columns, headed: "People," "Animals," "Places," and "Things."

  a. Give each student a card with two nouns written on it. Tell them to take turns to add their words to the chart, in the correct column.

  b. Invite students to add nouns to the chart at any convenient or transitional time during the day.

Exploring NOUNS

Alphabet Check

Give each student one letter of the alphabet. (Omit vowels and "x.") Ask each student to list five common nouns and five proper nouns beginning with the letter they have.

Share their lists with the whole class, ensuring that everyone understands why the given words are nouns—*Nouns name people, places, animals, and things.*

Check that proper names begin with capital letters.

Listen Up

Play "What am I?"
e.g.   I am red.
        I am crunchy.
        I am found in a tree.
        I begin with the letter "a."
        What am I?
        (*Answer:* apple)

Last One Standing

Divide the class into groups and play "Tops and Tails." The first player says a person's name. The next player then says another person's name. It must begin with the last letter of the name that the first player said. Play continues around the group. If a player cannot offer a name, they are "out." The winner is the last one standing.

Variation: Use names of animals, flowers, or birds instead of people's names.

Noun Hunt

Give each student a printed page from a magazine. Ask them to circle ten common nouns and five proper nouns. Give them a time limit of up to eight minutes. Share their findings. Ensure that everyone understands why the given words are nouns— Nouns name people, places, animals, and things.

The Veggie Patch

Divide the class into small groups. Give each group a letter of the alphabet. Their job is to list as many fruits and vegetables as they can, beginning with their letter. Invite them to use dictionaries. Each group could display and share their lists.

Noun Sorts

Place a chart on the wall, and divide the chart into two columns, headed "Common Nouns" and "Proper Nouns." Invite students to add one or two words to each column from a book they are reading. This should be an ongoing activity.

Nouns

Nouns name people, places, animals, and the everyday things around us.

1. Circle the four nouns in each sentence.

a. Brianna and her sister go to school by car.

b. My friend likes ice cream and jelly, but not custard.

c. The horse galloped up the hill, across the pasture, and over the fence.

2. Use all three nouns in a sentence.

a. Jacob, bus, town _____

_____

b. boat, fisherman, sea _____

_____

3. Add a noun to these sentences. The word in parentheses will help you.

a. An _____ is stamped on the back of a quarter.   (animal)

b. The farmer stores wheat in the _____.   (place)

c. I opened the box and there was a _____!   (thing)

d. My _____ is taller than I am.   (person)

4. Read the nouns in the boxes. Color the people <u>red</u>. Color the animals <u>blue</u>, the places <u>yellow</u>, and the things <u>green</u>.

prisoner	ladder	rabbit	beach	cloud	playground
statue	singer	office	dentist	bear	caterpillar

5.

a. Name three animals: _____

b. Name three places: _____

c. Name three persons: _____

d. Name three things: _____

Common Nouns

Common nouns name everyday people and things around us. (Examples: farmer, bus, goat, movie, cup, doctor, book, friend, bike)

1. **Underline the common nouns in these sentences. Draw a picture in the box about one of your answers.**

    a. We are waiting for the bus to come.

    b. This book is about snakes.

    c. My brother is riding his skateboard.

    d. A fly and a moth are caught in a web.

    e. There are knives, forks, and spoons on the table.

2. **How many common nouns can you find in each sentence?**

    a. The toddler drank the milk and ate the cookie.   _____

    b. Please go and stand by the window.   _____

    c. The man rode across the desert on his camel.   _____

    d. We walked together down the hill to school.   _____

    e. The teacher told us to open our books and write a story.   _____

3. **Let's pretend you are in a car driving along a country road. Name all the things you can see.**

    _____   _____   _____   _____

    _____   _____   _____   _____

    _____   _____   _____   _____

    _____   _____   _____   _____

NOUNS

Proper Nouns

Proper nouns give people, places, objects, and events their special names. (Examples: New York, Italy, T-mart, Hollywood, Nile River) Proper nouns always begin with a capital letter.

1. How many special names do you know? Write these proper nouns. (Don't forget to begin with a capital letter.)

a. a girl beginning with "t" _____

b. a city beginning with "p" _____

c. a brand of food _____

d. a famous building _____

e. a river _____

f. a place you visit _____

g. a month beginning with "j" _____

h. a day beginning with "t" _____

i. a country beginning with "a" _____

j. the name of a pet _____

k. a special event _____

l. a movie you have seen _____

2. Find the proper nouns in this text. Give them capital letters.

brian has a pen pal who lives in france. His name is jacques. jacques lives in the city of paris beside the river seine. brian and jacques both love to play soccer. One day jacques would like to visit brian in australia.

3. Choose your own proper nouns to complete this text.

_____ lives on a farm not far from the town of _____. He has a dog named _____. In the month of _____, when it is very hot, _____ gets on his bike and rides down to the _____ River nearby. _____ runs along behind. His friend _____ often meets him there. They always have a great time splashing about in the water. _____ barks and has a great time, too.

Singular and Plural Nouns

Nouns give names to all the things we speak and write about. We can name one thing (**singular noun**). (Examples: man, house, dish) Or, we can name more than one thing (**plural noun**). (Examples: men, houses, dishes)

NOUNS

1. Write these nouns in their correct columns.

cards   book   coat   carrot   coyotes

hen   bikes   flies   peaches   tub

Singular	Plural

2. Most plurals are formed by adding "s" or "es" to a singular noun. Write the plural form of these nouns.

a. bell _____

b. cake _____

c. box _____

d. branch _____

e. sock _____

f. pencil _____

g. kite _____

h. flower _____

i. calf* _____

j. baby* _____

Spelling alert!

3. Some plural nouns are not formed in this way. For example, *tooth* becomes *teeth*. Match these singular and plural nouns.

child   goose   mouse   foot   man

men   children   feet   geese   mice

NOUNS

Compound Nouns

A **compound noun** is made when two words are combined. (Examples: corn + flakes = cornflakes, foot + ball = football, snow + man = snowman)

1. Add a word from the box to each word in the list to make a compound noun.

drops	hole	ball	hill	light
case	fly	shell	watch	stairs

a. sun _____

b. down _____

c. man _____

d. base _____

e. ant _____

f. stop _____

g. rain _____

h. dragon _____

i. book _____

j. egg _____

2. Color the two words that make a compound word. Use a different color for each word.

table	tooth	card	ball	cloth	yard
paste	foot	box	post	farm	match

3. Write a sentence using each of these compound nouns.

a. scarecrow: _____

_____

b. windmill: _____

_____

c. bulldozer: _____

_____

Collective Nouns

Collective nouns are the names given to groups of people, animals, or things. (Examples: a <u>herd</u> of goats, a <u>fleet</u> of ships, a <u>school</u> of fish)

1. Search out the collective nouns. Use other resources to help you find the answers.

T	B	R	A	L	P	W	Z	Y	E
A	K	I	T	T	E	N	S	N	T
S	A	C	R	D	L	I	O	N	S
F	N	H	Y	B	E	R	S	Q	K
B	G	I	M	U	P	D	H	A	W
P	A	C	L	S	H	O	E	T	O
G	R	K	B	P	A	M	E	F	L
R	O	E	J	R	N	C	P	R	V
U	O	N	X	G	T	V	Y	T	E
B	S	S	U	M	S	B	E	E	S

CLUES

a. a litter of k _____

b. a herd of e _____

c. a brood of ch _____

d. a pack of w _____

e. a mob of k _____

f. a flock of sh _____

g. a swarm of b _____

h. a pride of l _____

2. Circle the collective nouns in this text.

A crowd of people gathered along the seashore. They waited patiently to photograph the pod of whales moving slowly northward. A school of fish swam by, as well as a school of porpoises. A flock of seagulls screeched noisily overhead. After several hours, a cheer went up. The pod of whales had finally arrived!

3. Draw one of the following:

- an army of frogs
- a colony of rabbits
- a troop of monkeys
- a cloud of flies
- a convoy of trucks

NOUNS

Possessive Nouns

Possessive nouns show ownership. We use an apostrophe to show possession. (Examples: Claire's shoes, cat's whiskers, boy's hat, hen's feathers, teachers' books)

If there is one owner, just add **'s.**	If there is more than one owner, put an apostrophe after the plural noun.	If the plural noun does not end in "s," add **'s.**

the <u>man's</u> hat (the hat belonging to the man)	the <u>girls'</u> cats (the cats belonging to the girls)	the <u>children's</u> kites (the kites belonging to the children)

1. Rewrite each sentence using apostrophes to show possession.

 a. The horse belongs to Danielle. It is Danielle's horse.

 b. The car belongs to Mr. Tan. It _____

 c. The web belongs to a spider. It _____

 d. The bones belong to the dinosaur. They _____

 e. The nests belong to the birds. They _____

 f. The golf balls belong to the men. They _____

2. Who owns the objects that are underlined in these sentences?

 a. It is the builder's <u>toolbox</u>. the builder

 b. Owls' <u>eyes</u> peered in the dark. _____

 c. There is the farmer's <u>field</u>. _____

 d. We ate the women's <u>cakes</u>. _____

 e. I patted my friend's <u>dogs</u>. _____

 f. These are Emily's <u>shorts</u>. _____

3. Write a sentence about the dragons' cave or the witch's frogs.

_____

Verbal Nouns

Some forms of a verb can be used as a noun. These are called **verbal nouns**. They end in *-ing*. (Examples: <u>Walking</u> is good exercise. <u>Hurling</u> is an Irish sport.)

1. Circle the verbal noun in each sentence.

   a. Racing is a dangerous sport.

   b. My friend does kickboxing.

   c. My uncle sometimes takes me birdwatching.

   d. Stargazing is a fascinating hobby.

   e. Pruning roses makes the plants produce better flowers.

2. Match these sentences.

a. Reading	of paper folding.
b. You will need special boots	for stamp collecting.
c. Mom put seasoning	is my favorite pastime.
d. Origami is the art	to go rock climbing.
e. Tom has a large album	in the meat stew.

3. Write in each blank the correct verbal noun. Add any capital letters that are needed.

   a. _____ is difficult in the center of the city.

   b. _____ on the street is dangerous.

   c. The sport of _____ began in France.

   d. My grandma loves _____.

   e. There is not enough _____ on our street.

fencing
playing
lighting
parking
knitting

NOUNS

Noun Phrases

A group of words built around a noun is called a **noun phrase**. They point out the people and things being spoken or written about. (Examples: the big, black spider; my best friend; his new bike; the runaway horse)

1. Write some noun phrases using the words in the box.

monkey	the	chair	sneaky	car	his	brown
red	dog	my	little	kitchen	clean	fast

his little red car _____   _____

_____   _____

_____   _____

2. Build your own noun phrases.

a. my _____ slippers

b. the _____ forest

c. this _____

d. the _____ elephant

e. her _____ books

f. a _____

3. Complete the noun phrases with words of your own choice.

a. the wide and dusty _____   *e.* the bright, sparkling _____

b. a long, yellow _____   *f.* a wet and windy _____

c. my playful _____   *g.* the shy, brown _____

d. a crunchy, juicy, red _____   *h.* the soft, green _____

4. Write three sentences to include these noun phrases.

a long, black shadow   a brown, leather football   a baggy, clown costume

a. _____

b. _____

c. _____

Nouns with Suffixes

Many nouns have **suffixes**, which are special word endings. (Examples: content<u>ment</u>, sad<u>ness</u>, impress<u>ion</u>, mother<u>hood</u>, serv<u>ant</u>, drumm<u>er</u>)

NOUNS

| appoint \ **ment** | selfish \ **ness** | box \ **er** |

1. Write the noun that is made by adding the noun suffix.

a. teach + er =   teacher

b. move + ment = _____

c. soft + ness = _____

d. good + ness = _____

e. build + er = _____

f. wonder + ment = _____

2. Choose the correct suffix to change these words into nouns.

| –ment   –ness   –er |

a. great_____   *d.* bank_____   *g.* apart_____

b. play_____   *e.* amuse_____   *h.* fair_____

c. entertain_____   *f.* kind_____   *i.* photograph_____

3. Write the missing words. Choose from the nouns in the box.

| drummer   appointment   gentleness   refreshments   darkness |

a. He peered into the _____, trying to see where the noise had come from.

b. Jane has an _____ with the dentist at three o'clock.

c. After the football game, the players were served _____.

d. She spoke with such _____, the baby stopped crying immediately.

e. When I grow up, I want to be a _____ in a band.

4. Write a sentence about a swimmer, a dancer, or a horseback rider.

_____

_____

A word about ARTICLES

- "A" and "an" are only used with <u>singular</u> nouns. They are <u>indefinite</u> because they point to something that is not known by the reader or the listener.

- "A" is used before a word beginning with a <u>consonant</u>. (Examples: a rose, a computer, a clever girl)

- "An" is used before a word beginning with a <u>vowel</u>. (Examples: an orange, an odd noise, an igloo)

- "An" is also used before a word beginning with an "h" (not sounded). (Examples: an hour, an honor)

- "The" is a <u>definite</u> article because it points to something that has been made known to the reader or listener. (Examples: the cap I wear, the ball in the box)

- "The" is always used before <u>plural</u> nouns. (Examples: the eggs in the nest, the children at school)

- "The" is also used when it points to a common noun known by everyone. (Examples: the sun, the morning)

NOTE: A character in a story is usually introduced as "a." (Examples: There was once <u>a</u> giant, <u>a</u> red fox, <u>a</u> beautiful princess, <u>a</u> brave knight)

Once the character has been introduced, they can be referred to as "the."
(Examples: <u>The</u> giant spoke, <u>The</u> red fox prowled, <u>The</u> princess lived)

Articles 1

Three **articles** are used to signal nouns or noun phrases:

a   an   the

NOUNS

1. Read the following story and fill in the blanks with the articles "a," "an," or "the."

Once there was _____ wild horse. It was snowy white with _____ long flowing mane. _____ horse could sometimes be seen in _____ late afternoon, just before _____ sun went down. Then it would disappear into _____ dark, rocky cave. One day, _____ adventurer who had been walking in _____ hills was looking for _____ cave where he might sleep for _____ night. Behind _____ large shelf of rock, he found _____ small cave. It was _____ cave where _____ white horse lived. He went inside. He stopped with _____ gasp at _____ sight before him. Rays of light, streaming from _____ hole in _____ cave roof, fell upon _____ white horse. It shone like silver in _____ soft light.

2. Write a noun phrase to follow these articles.

a. a _____

b. an _____

c. the _____ (singular)

d. the _____ (plural)

e. an _____

f. a _____

3. Write three facts about a horse or a bear. When you have finished, circle all the articles you used.

_____

_____

_____

_____

_____

_____

Articles 2

The **articles** "a," "an," and "the" are often used to introduce nouns or noun phrases. (Examples: a car, an excellent adventure, the owl and the pussycat)

NOUNS

1. Write whether the underlined articles are definite (D) or indefinite (I).

a. As I looked at <u>the</u> sky, I saw <u>a</u> bird land in the tree. _____ _____

b. <u>The</u> bird then hopped along <u>the</u> branch to its nest. _____ _____

c. From <u>the</u> nest, I could hear <u>a</u> baby bird chirping. _____ _____

d. <u>The</u> mother bird fed <u>the</u> baby, then flew away. _____ _____

2. "A," "an," and "the" signal nouns or noun phrases. Circle the noun phrases in these sentences.

a. A sleepy, blue-tongue lizard lay on the warm, brown rocks.

b. An old and wise woman told Jack to plant the bean seeds.

c. I put the fresh strawberries in a green plastic basket.

d. The frightened horse jumped the wire fence.

e. He gave me a chocolate Easter egg.

3. Use "a" or "an" before the following words.

a. _____ dream

b. _____ oven

c. _____ yacht

d. _____ axe

e. _____ ostrich

f. _____ quest

g. _____ iron

h. _____ island

i. _____ answer

j. _____ parrot

k. _____ piano

l. _____ avocado

m. _____ potato

n. _____ hour

o. _____ inning

p. _____ pumpkin

Assessment - Nouns

CHECK 1: Underline the word in each group that is NOT a noun. ☐ /5

a. <u>quiet</u>   ribbon   pie

b. garden   goal   going

c. fast   house   floor

d. herd   dollar   pretty

e. lunch   tall   bridge

f. zebra   clown   angry

CHECK 2: Circle all the nouns in this text. ☐ /10

James and Byron built a clubhouse in Byron's garden. They used boards, nailed to a branch, for the floor. They strung up old sheets for the walls and the roof.

CHECK 3: Write a noun from the text above that is: ☐ /4

a. common_____

b. proper_____

c. possessive_____

d. compound_____

CHECK 4: Write six compound words using the words in the box. ☐ /6

(Words can be used more than once.)

day	junk	house	water	farm	side	sun
yard	time	light	life	back	play	line

a. _____

b. _____

c. _____

d. _____

e. _____

f. _____

CHECK 5: Write the plural form of these nouns. ☐ /5

a. bus   b. plate   c. day   d. baby   e. leaf

_____   _____   _____   _____   _____

CHECK 6: Add the correct suffix to these words to make nouns. ☐ /5

–ness	–er	–ment

a. sweet_____   b. amuse_____   c. garden_____   d. great_____   e. amaze_____

Assessment - Nouns

CHECK 7: Underline the noun phrases in this text.   ☐ /5

> The colorful clown squeezed into the tiny red car. He drove
> slowly around the large circus ring. Suddenly, he threw open a
> huge green umbrella. All of the people laughed and cheered.

CHECK 8: Rewrite these sentences using possessive nouns.   ☐ /5

a. She washed <u>the dress belonging to Sunita</u>.

_____

b. Milk drips from <u>the whiskers belonging to the cat</u>.

_____

c. Isaac cleaned <u>the cars belonging to the teachers</u>.

_____

d. <u>The boots belonging to the workers</u> are very muddy.

_____

e. <u>The wings belonging to the fly</u> beat silently.

_____

CHECK 9: Write three or four sentences about your school. When you have finished, go back and underline five nouns in your sentences.   ☐ /5

_____

_____

_____

_____

_____

_____

Student Name: _____

Date: _____   Total Score: _____/50

ADJECTIVES

Adjectives are words that give color, shape, size, sound, and feeling to nouns. Their job is to paint clearer pictures of nouns.

A Note to the Teacher

Speakers and writers create images of people and things through their choice of **adjectives**.

Adjectives give meaning and life to nouns. They are often chosen specifically to give a positive or a negative view of people, places, events, and objects.

Advertisers know this very well, and they choose adjectives that will display their products in the most desirable way. They use words like *reliable, charming, immaculate, heavy-duty,* etc. Value can be *outstanding, great,* or *unbeatable.*

The media, too, selects adjectives designed to sway the audience to a particular view. Of a dictator it may use words like *evil, vicious, ruthless,* and the acts of such a person may be described as *despicable, brutal,* or *inhuman.* Whereas a princess may be described as *beautiful, stylish, graceful,* performing acts that are *generous, compassionate,* and *admirable.*

Adjectives give life and personality to all the people and things we speak and write about.

Carl, a <u>tall</u> man, went to the <u>local</u> shop to buy <u>big</u> bones for his <u>shaggy</u>, <u>brown</u> dog.

Adjectives are very powerful tools used by writers and speakers.

Adjectives can be placed before the noun they describe.

e.g., I stroked the <u>soft</u> fur of the <u>tiny</u>, <u>white</u> kitten.

Adjectives can be placed after the noun they describe.

e.g., The door was <u>wooden</u> and <u>heavy</u>. This orange is <u>sweet</u> and <u>juicy</u>.

Different adjectives have different jobs to do.

Descriptive adjectives give color, shape, size, and feeling to nouns.

e.g., <u>sharp</u> pencil; <u>choppy</u> seas; <u>haunting</u> melody; <u>scruffy</u> dog; <u>long</u>, <u>dusty</u> road; <u>quaint</u>, <u>whitewashed</u> cottages

Verbal adjectives are participles used as adjectives. Participles end in *–ing* or *–ed.*

e.g., a <u>walking</u> stick; <u>falling</u> rocks; a <u>deafening</u> roar; <u>scented</u> roses; a <u>puzzled</u> look; a <u>dazed</u> expression

Number adjectives give quantity to the noun.

e.g., <u>ten</u> geese; <u>five</u> marbles; <u>sixth</u> person; <u>first</u> place

Indefinite adjectives give an uncertain quantity to the noun.

e.g., <u>some</u> children; <u>few</u> coins; <u>many</u> soldiers; <u>most</u> people

Adjectives of degree may describe nouns as they are (positive degree).

e.g., I have a <u>long</u> rope.

Or, they may be compared to another (comparative degree).

e.g., My rope is <u>longer</u> than yours.

Or, they may be compared to all others (superlative degree).

e.g., Todd has the <u>longest</u> rope of all.

Suffixes *–er* and *–est* are usually used to make adjectives of degree.

e.g., old, older, oldest; sweet, sweeter, sweetest

Other adjectives of degree are formed by placing *more* or *most* before the adjective.

More and *most* are used before adjectives that already end in a suffix.

e.g., beautiful, more beautiful, most beautiful; helpful, more helpful, most helpful; famous, more famous, most famous

Similes

Adjectives are used in similes—figures of speech which likens one thing to another—to provide a clearer word picture of something or someone. The words *as* and *like* are used.

e.g., as light as a feather; as cold as ice; as white as snow

Adjectives show opposite ways of describing nouns. Because the work of adjectives is to describe nouns, it is possible to use them in ways that will give opposite views of people and things. These adjectives are called **antonyms**.

e.g., a short/tall person; fresh/stale cake; sweet/sour oranges; dull/bright day; rough/smooth road

Adjective-forming suffixes

A suffix (word ending) changes the way a word is used in a sentence. Some suffixes added to words form adjectives (e.g., funny, helpful, careless, comfortable, famous, tiresome, attractive, foolish, dependent).

Ideas for introducing adjectives

- Ask the students to name some familiar objects in the room (e.g., clock, desk, chair, book door, pencil) and make a list on the side of the board.

- Select one object and write a "bare bones" sentences on the board (e.g., The book is on the shelf.)

- Ask the students to give you a word that you could add to describe the book, to say what it looks like (e.g., large).

- Rewrite the sentence:

  (e.g., The large book is on the shelf.)

  Invite the students to think of other words, and write them in a list underneath *large*. Prompt the students with thoughts of color, size, weight, content, etc. Ask different students to read the new sentences.

- Introduce the word *adjective*, a word used to describe a noun. Writers (and speakers) use them to paint pictures of people and things they are talking about. Readers (and listeners) will get a much clearer picture of a person, place, or thing if you paint a good picture.

  Adjectives will help you do this.

- Repeat the process above with the word *shelf*.

- Ask the students to write any one combination of sentences you have just studied.

- Write this sentence on the board:

  The little boy jumped over the high wall.

Invite the students to write four or five different sentences changing only the words *little* and *high*. Share the results.

- Ask the students to select another word from the list of familiar objects. Ask them to write a "bare bones" sentence, and then list some adjectives they could add to paint a better picture of each noun. Have them share their work.

- Discuss how we tend to describe things by using our senses—seeing, hearing, touching, smelling, tasting—and by the way we feel inside. Ask the students to describe an object using their different senses. See the examples below.

seeing (a man): tall, stooped, old, tired, busy

hearing (an insect): buzzing, chirping, singing, hissing, whining

tasting (a fruit): sweet, juicy, sour, crunchy, tangy, bitter

touching (a stone): rough, smooth, coarse, cold, gritty

smelling (a room): musty, fresh, smoky, stinking, dusty

feelings: angry, happy, glum, sad, glad, excited

- Tell students that using their senses will help them to think of the adjectives that will best describe the people, places, and things they are writing (or speaking) about.

Exploring ADJECTIVES

Adjectives in the News

Invite the students to work in pairs with the real estate section of a newspaper. Together they should list the adjectives used by advertisers to "sell" their houses.

e.g., neat and tidy, wonderful [entertainment area], stunning [views], freshly-painted

Share their findings. Discuss the similarities in the language chosen for this form of advertising.

Variation: Explore other forms of "persuasive" advertising in the car section, fashion magazine, sporting equipment, etc.

Adjectives Alert

Ask the students to list all the adjectives they can find in the first two pages of a book that they are reading. As an extension, they could write beside each adjective the noun it describes.

Collections

Divide the class into small groups. Supply each group with magazines, papers, junk mail, etc. Nominate a topic for each group (e.g., sports, clothes, cars, animals, food, men, women, children, holidays, etc.).

Ask each group to find and paste pictures about their topic onto a sheet of paper. Ask them to write any number of describing adjectives under each picture.

Have each group present their sheet and place it on display in the room.

Choice Language

Make an enlarged copy of a piece of text containing a number of adjectives. White-out up to ten adjectives and make copies for each student.

Ask the students to write adjectives in the spaces. Have them share their work.

Discuss the similarities and differences in the "pictures" created by their choices.

As an extension, ask half the class to write from a positive point of view and the other half from a negative one.

Share the resulting texts and discuss.

Picture Perfect

Invite the students to paste several small pictures from a magazine into books. There should be a mix of people, animals, places, and objects. Below each one, ask them to write a noun phrase that includes at least one adjective (e.g., a tasty pizza; a shiny car; crunchy, red apples).

Descriptive Adjectives

Adjectives are words we use to describe nouns. (Examples: a <u>blue</u> sky; a <u>large</u> river; <u>tasty</u> food; a <u>noisy</u> truck; a <u>beautiful</u> lady; <u>rough</u> roads)

Adjectives and nouns work together to give clear pictures of people, places, and things.

Adjectives give shape, size, sound, color, and feeling to nouns.

1. **We can place an adjective in front of the noun that we want to describe. Write an adjective in each space to describe the noun.**

   a. We had _____ soup for lunch.

   b. I gave the boy a _____ cookie to eat.

   c. The girl is brushing her _____ hair.

   d. The _____ soldier stumbled back to camp.

   e. I heard a _____ noise coming from the _____ house.

2. **We can place an adjective after the noun we want to describe. Circle the adjectives that describe the underlined nouns.**

   a. My <u>mother</u> is pretty.

   b. The <u>horse</u> was young and frisky.

   c. An <u>elephant</u> is strong.

   d. The <u>man</u> was old and gray.

   e. <u>Helen</u> is tall and thin.

3. **The adjectives are underlined. Draw arrows to show which nouns they describe.**

   a. The <u>tired</u> man said the box was <u>heavy</u>.

   b. The boy was <u>sorry</u> he missed the <u>exciting</u> football game.

   c. The night was <u>dark</u>, and the road was <u>long</u>.

   d. My dog was <u>happy</u> to get a <u>great</u>, <u>big</u> bone to eat.

   e. The <u>young</u> girl spoke to the <u>kind</u> and <u>friendly</u> teacher.

Number Adjectives

Adjectives show number. (Examples: <u>six</u> boys, <u>two</u> hens, <u>first</u> place, <u>two</u> hundred dollars, <u>last</u> chance)

1. **Complete the noun phrases using words from the box. Include at least one describing adjective. (Example: seven <u>silly stories</u>)**

If we are unsure of the exact number, we use the following words: *some, few, many, most.*

noisy	rabbits	lonely	stories	peaches	dogs	silly
people	funny	ants	busy	hens	jokes	clowns

a. four _____

b. a few _____

c. eleven _____

d. most _____

e. some _____

f. two _____

g. many _____

h. sixty _____

2. **Color the size adjectives <u>green</u>, the shape adjectives <u>blue</u>, the sound adjectives <u>yellow</u>, and the feeling adjectives <u>red</u>.**

angry	quiet	tiny	loud	excited	tall
noisy	oval	lazy	square	large	round

3. **Sort the adjectives into the correct columns below.**

smooth   bright   hairy   juicy   sweet   soft

multicolored   sour   uneven   windy   tangy   pretty

Taste	Touch	Sight

Antonyms

Because adjectives are describing words, we can use them to describe people and things in a totally opposite way. (Examples: a long street/a short street; fresh bread/stale bread; happy girls/sad girls; old books/new books; a tall man/a short man)

Adjectives that give opposite viewpoints are called **antonyms**.

ADJECTIVES

1. Write, and then search for, the antonyms (opposites) of these adjectives.

fast _____

noisy _____

young _____

sad _____

tall _____

light _____

smooth _____

ugly _____

low _____

above _____

S	F	P	T	N	C	J	O	K	R
D	B	B	E	L	O	W	X	L	B
Y	E	G	Y	P	F	Q	I	H	D
U	A	N	V	O	Z	U	V	G	L
N	U	R	A	R	B	I	T	U	P
S	T	Z	E	L	T	E	F	O	K
H	I	G	H	Q	R	T	M	R	L
O	F	A	E	P	O	W	G	J	G
W	U	T	R	Y	H	A	P	P	Y
S	L	O	W	X	S	H	S	A	D

2. Write antonyms for these adjectives.

a. clean _____

b. top _____

c. first _____

d. empty _____

e. slow _____

f. wet _____

3. Complete these sentences by using the correct antonyms.

a. The bucket was _____ , but now it is _____.

b. My clothes were _____ , but now they are _____.

c. A rabbit is _____, but a tortoise is _____.

d. He fell from the _____ step to the _____.

Verbal Adjectives

Some forms of a verb can be used as adjectives. They are called **verbal adjectives**. They end in *–ing* or *–ed*. (Examples: a <u>walking</u> stick, <u>falling</u> rocks, a <u>winding</u> road, <u>loaded</u> trucks, a <u>puzzled</u> look)

ADJECTIVES

1. Join these verbal adjectives to the nouns they describe.

a. dancing	rocks	*g.* scented	shoes
b. an exciting	clouds	*h.* loaded	nuts
c. swimming	book	*i.* baked	cream
d. falling	shoes	*j.* polished	rose
e. an interesting	suit	*k.* mixed	truck
f. floating	day	*l.* whipped	pies

2. Use three of the noun phrases above in sentences.

a. _____

b. _____

c. _____

3. Make a sketch of each noun phrase.

a smiling clown	a parked car	splashing waves	a potted plant
a jumping rope	a painted face	a walking stick	a speckled hen

Adjectives of Degree

Adjectives of degree describe how people and things compare with each other. They show how much more or less. (Example: John is <u>tall</u>. Owen is <u>taller</u>. Martin is <u>tallest</u>.) To show degree we usually add *–er* and *–est*.

1. Color the matching adjectives of degree. Use a different color for each set.

Adjective	Comparative	Superlative
loud	wetter	strongest
tall	thinner	loudest
fierce	louder	fiercest
wet	stronger	wettest
thin	fiercer	tallest
strong	taller	thinnest

2. Complete the table of adjectives of degree.

Adjectives	Comparative	Superlative
long	longer	longest
old		
sharp		
wild		
soft		
brave		

3. Complete the adjectives of degree correctly. Add *–er* or *–est*.

  a. That was the cold_____ day in winter.

  b. It is warm_____ today than it was yesterday.

  c. My grandma is old_____ than yours.

  d. Jordan is the fast_____ runner in our class.

  e. The red box is large, but the blue one is larg_____.

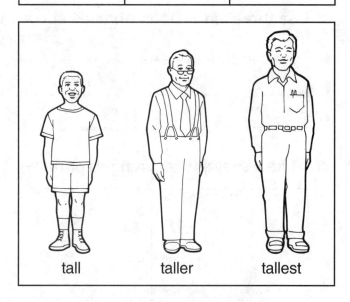

tall   taller   tallest

4. Some adjectives of degree are not formed by adding *–er* or *–est*. (Examples: good, better, best; bad, worse, worst) Write two sentences that include some of these adjectives.

  a. _____

  b. _____

ADJECTIVES

Adjectives with Suffixes

Many adjectives have **suffixes**—special word endings. (Examples: person<u>al</u>, juic<u>y</u>, ac<u>tive</u>, tox<u>ic</u>, fool<u>ish</u>, fashion<u>able</u>, deli<u>cious</u>)

help	ful
help	less
like	able

1. Add the correct suffix to complete the sentence.

| –able | –ful | –less |

a. Be care_____ ! Don't drop the eggs.

b. My bed is very comfort_____.

c. They had a wonder_____ time at the party.

d. The travelers crossed a tree_____ desert.

e. These new jeans have an adjust_____ belt.

2. Write the two adjectives made by adding the suffixes –ful and –less.

a. use_____   b. cheer_____   c. shame_____   d. mind_____

   use_____   cheer_____   shame_____   mind_____

3. Think of a noun that can be described by these adjectives.

a. something comfortable to wear   _____

b. someone who is youthful   _____

c. something useful in the kitchen   _____

d. something careless you might do   _____

e. something wonderful to do   _____

f. a place that is restful   _____

g. something drinkable   _____

h. something measured by the spoonful   _____

i. something colorful   _____

j. something old and useless   _____

Adjectives in Similes

Adjectives are often used in **similes**. Similes paint a clear picture by showing how one thing is like something else. The words *as* and *like* are used. (Examples: as cold as ice, as old as the hills, as flat as a pancake)

1. Circle the simile in each sentence.

a. Dad told me to be as quiet as a mouse.

b. She was as busy as a bee in the garden.

c. The road was as straight as an arrow.

d. Last night the sky was as black as ink.

e. Her face was as pale as a ghost.

2. Complete these similes using words from the box.

a. as gentle as a _____

b. as light as a _____

c. as sick as a _____

d. as pretty as a _____

e. as white as _____

f. as cool as a _____

g. as blind as a _____

snow
picture
bat
cucumber
feather
dog
lamb

3. Write some similes of your own.

a. Her eyes are as blue as _____.

b. This chair is as hard as _____.

c. The villagers were as poor as _____.

d. My shoes are as shiny as _____.

e. The river is as wide as _____.

f. She felt as young as a _____.

g. The moon is as silent as _____.

h. That was as funny as _____.

4. Choose any simile and use it in a sentence.

_____

_____

Assessment - Adjectives

CHECK 1: Cross out the adjective in each row that does NOT describe the noun. ☐ /5

a. apple	sweet	snowy	crunchy	red
b. sky	bright	blue	stinky	cloudy
c. sandwich	plastic	cheese	fresh	tasty
d. boot	white	leather	sore	fancy
e. fire	smoky	wet	fierce	cozy

CHECK 2: Sort the adjectives below into the correct columns. ☐ /12

foggy	crunchy	plastic	round	cheerful	damp
smiling	rocky	worried	careless	sandy	thick

People	Places	Things

CHECK 3: Circle all the adjectives. ☐ /10

   a. The lady I saw was slim with blonde hair.

   b. The rescue team threw a rope to the trapped miner.

   c. I read a frightening story about a haunted house.

   d. The pilot took off on his first solo flight.

   e. In the sea, I found a box of gold coins and sparkling jewels.

CHECK 4: Write the antonyms (opposites) of these adjectives. ☐ /8

   a. high _____   **e.** dangerous _____

   b. careful _____   **f.** smooth _____

   c. beautiful _____   **g.** full _____

   d. small _____   **h.** narrow _____

ADJECTIVES

Assessment - Adjectives

CHECK 5: **Complete the similes. Use one in a sentence.** ☐ /5

  a. as white as _____   *c.* as heavy as _____

  b. as pretty as a _____   *d.* as light as a _____

  _____

  _____

ADJECTIVES

CHECK 6: **Add the correct suffix from the box.** ☐ /5

–able	–ful	–less

  a. bear_____

  b. harm_____

  c. hand_____

  d. cord_____

  e. pass_____

CHECK 7: **Complete the adjectives of degree.** ☐ /5

  a. Tammy is a fast_____ runner than Mary.

  b. Death Valley is one of the hot_____ places on Earth.

  c. I am good at math, but Todd is much _____.

  d. We will need a strong_____ rope than this one.

  e. That was the hard_____ game I have ever played.

Student Name: _____

Date: _____   Total Score: _____/50

PRONOUNS

Pronouns are the words that are used instead of nouns in text. They can be singular or plural, masculine or feminine, and they do the same work as nouns.

Texts, both spoken and written, are made up of sentences whose ideas connect to each other in meaningful ways.

Pronouns are used to replace nouns to avoid the monotony of repetition.

Sarah lost her hat in the park. Mark said that he would help her look for it. She said that it was bright red, so they should find it easily.

These pronouns refer back to nouns already mentioned and give the text fluency and cohesion.

First-person pronouns are used when a writer, a speaker, or a character is doing the "talking."

e.g., I eat my greens.

Second-person pronouns are used when someone is spoken to.

e.g., If you look, you will see your hat.

Third-person pronouns are used when a writer or speaker talks about other people and things.

e.g., They left them behind with their teacher.

Different pronouns have different jobs to do.

Personal pronouns replace the names of the people, places, animals, and everyday things around us.

- First-person pronouns are:
  I, me, my, mine, we, us, our, ours

- Second-person pronouns are:
  you, your, yours

- Third-person pronouns are:
  he, his, him, she, her, hers, it, its, they, them, their, theirs

Possessive pronouns show ownership. No apostrophes are needed.

These pronouns are as follows: *my, mine, our, ours, your, yours, hers, its, their, theirs*

Interrogative pronouns are used to ask certain questions—Who? Whom? (rarely used) Whose? Which? What?

e.g., Who ate all the cakes?

Whom did you see?

Whose books are on the floor?

Which bus do you catch?

What is your address?

Ideas for introducing pronouns

- Write two sentences on the board, the second using one or two pronouns.

  e.g., The girl has a jump rope.
  <u>She</u> likes to play with <u>it</u>.

- Ask to whom the "she" and the "it" refer. Use arrows to show the link between "she" and "girl" and "it" and "jump rope." Write and discuss other examples using different personal pronouns.

- Introduce the term *pronouns*—words that take the place of nouns. Discuss the reason for using pronouns instead of repeating the nouns.

- Point out that pronouns usually refer <u>back</u> to nouns in the text.

  Sometimes pronouns do point forward.

  e.g., "We can't come with you," said Jasmine and Fay together.

- Begin a list of personal pronouns with the students' help. You may wish to list them under first-, second-, and third-person pronouns.

- Give the students a short piece of magazine (or other) text, and give them five minutes to locate the pronouns that have been used. Share their findings.

- Do some oral cloze activities.

  e.g., The dog bit the mailman, and _____ began to cry.

  Rowan and Cal have skateboards.
  _____ go to the skate park every day.

Exploring PRONOUNS

The Pros and Cons

Select a piece of text and make an enlarged copy. White-out ten pronouns. Make copies for each child (or pair). Ask them to write the pronouns into the spaces. Share answers.

Variation: White-out ten nouns instead. Ask the students to fill in what the nouns might be, using the pronouns as their clue. Make sure they understand that there will be no one "right" answer for every noun missing.

I Spy

Ask the students to record all the pronouns they can find in the first ten lines of a book that they are reading. As an extension, ask them also to record which noun each pronoun has replaced. Share their findings.

Make the Connection

Hand each student two or three index cards containing nouns (singular, plural, and possessive). In turn, ask the students what pronouns they would use to replace the nouns on their cards.

e.g., boat (it), Mrs. Jackson (she), Tammy and Mia (they), Jai's (his)

Pronoun Sorts

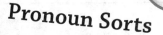

Give pairs of students a piece of copied text or a magazine article. Ask them to cut out ten pronouns each and group them in some way (e.g., singular and plural; personal and possessive; or first-, second-, and third-person). Tell them to paste their groups on a piece of paper. Share and display their work.

Speak Up

Ask students to cut pictures of two people out of a magazine and paste them, facing each other, in their notebooks. Show students how to draw a large speech bubble above each person. Invite them to write what each person might be saying to the other. Check later to see what pronouns they have used.

Personal Pronouns

Pronouns are used instead of nouns in speaking and writing. **Personal pronouns** replace the names of people and things.

PRONOUNS

I me my mine
you your yours
she her hers
he him his
it its
they their them theirs
we us our ours

1. Circle the pronouns in each sentence.

a. Pass me the biscuits, please.

b. They like jelly beans.

c. Wait for her at the bus stop.

d. I gave him a bag of marbles.

e. We didn't see them at the pool.

2. Replace the underlined noun with a pronoun, then complete the sentence.

a. Jane is a great tennis player.

She _____

_____

b. Maria opened the last birthday present.

_____

_____

c. The door is a heavy wooden one.

_____

_____

d. Don, Sam, and Abdul are watching television.

_____

_____

3. Find the pronouns and circle them.

they	me	her
we	she	them
their	us	you
your	my	he

s	m	e	r	h	e	r	p
o	t	h	e	m	l	o	d
w	e	z	f	t	h	e	y
k	p	s	h	e	t	n	j
t	h	e	i	r	b	c	s
n	y	o	u	r	d	n	q
u	s	n	m	a	h	e	x
b	z	h	y	s	u	w	k

4. Sketch the following.

my teddy bear	your face	our room	his pet rabbit

©Teacher Created Resources, Inc.

Pronouns – Number and Gender

Personal pronouns can be singular, plural, male, and female. Pronouns are male, female, or neutral, depending on the nouns they replace.
Singular: I, he, she, her, him, his, it
Plural: we, us, our, ours, they, them, their, theirs
Singular and plural: you, your, yours

1. Write (S) beside the singular pronouns and (P) beside the plural pronouns.

a. I (   ) asked them (   ) to sit down and talk to me (   ).

b. "Hello, Jess. Do you (   ) know where they (   ) have all gone?"

c. He (   ) told her (   ) not to go with them (   ).

2. Circle the correct pronoun.

a. Give the children (them, their) lunch now.

b. (Him, He) took a dollar from (his, him) pocket.

c. That bag of marbles is (my, mine).

d. Daniel is putting on (his, her) football jersey.

e. The magpie flapped (their, its) wings.

3. One pronoun has been underlined. Write the noun it replaces on the line.

a. "Will <u>you</u> make a cake?" Samantha asked her mother. _____

b. Bess pointed to the boys and said, "<u>They</u> are making a raft." _____

c. "Will you give <u>me</u> a jelly bean, please?" asked Sean. _____

d. "Let <u>us</u> build a tree house," said Debbie to her friend. _____

e. John gave me the book and said, "Please put <u>it</u> on the shelf." _____

4. Write four sentences using these pairs of pronouns.

she, her	you, him	they, them	we, it

a. _____

b. _____

c. _____

d. _____

PRONOUNS

PRONOUNS

Possessive Pronouns

Possessive pronouns show ownership. No apostrophe is needed. Look at the examples below.

my book (mine)	*his boat (his)*	*their dog (theirs)*
our pets (ours)	*her doll (hers)*	*your smile (yours)*

1. Circle the possessive pronouns.

a. Cody gave his mother a bunch of flowers.

b. The ball on the roof is mine.

c. Give the pencil back to Dana. It is hers.

d. We rode our horses in their paddock.

e. Put your books on my table, please.

2. Choose the correct possessive pronoun.

yours	their	ours	his	mine

a. Tim fed _____ pet rabbit.

b. We have paid for the ball, so it is _____.

c. If this hat is _____, come and get it, please.

d. The children took their homework assignment to _____ teacher.

e. That ruler is _____. Please give it back to me.

3. Complete the sentences with your own ideas.

a. After we had our lunch, _____.

b. Put your _____.

c. On the last day of their vacation, _____

_____.

A word about PUNCTUATION

RULES	**EXAMPLES**

Capital letters are used for the following:

- the first word in a sentence. — *<u>Come</u> to the circus with me.*

- proper names. — *<u>Cinderella</u> danced with <u>Prince Charming</u>.*

- the first spoken word in dialogue. — *He said, "<u>Let's</u> play soccer."*

- to emphasize important words. — *You did <u>WHAT</u>?*

Periods end statements and commands. — *That is a fine straw hat.*
Put it on, please.

Question marks end questions. — *How long will you be away?*

Exclamation marks end exclamations. — *What! Late again!*

Commas are used for the following:

- to separate words in a list. — *I like apples, pears, plums, and grapes.*

- to separate a beginning phrase. — *Later that day, we went for a swim.*

- to separate a beginning clause. — *When I broke my leg, I used crutches.*

- to separate an embedded phrase. — *Jess, waving her umbrella, hurried away.*

- to separate an embedded clause. — *My dog, which is old now, still does tricks.*

- to separate spoken and unspoken words. — *"A dingo is a wild dog," said Bradley.*

Quotation marks are used around spoken words. — *"<u>Dinner is on the table</u>," called Brenda.*
"<u>Thank you</u>," Jess replied.
(Remember: New speaker, new line.)

Apostrophes are used for the following:

- with nouns to show possession. — *<u>Joel's</u> toys, <u>dog's</u> collar,*
<u>teachers'</u> staff room

- in contractions with pronouns and helping verbs. — *<u>I've</u> packed lunch. <u>You're</u> invited. <u>It's</u> fun.*

- in contractions with helping verbs and negatives. — *He <u>can't</u> swim. I <u>couldn't</u> sing. <u>Don't</u> shout.*

Interrogative Pronouns

Some pronouns are used to ask questions, such as:
Who? Which? What? Whose? Whom?

PRONOUNS

1. Answer these questions.

a. What do you like for breakfast? _____

b. Who is your best friend? _____

c. Whose house is next door to yours? _____

d. Which TV show do you like best? _____

2. Write four questions and ask a friend to answer them.

a. Who _____

_____

b. Which _____

_____

c. What _____

_____

d. Whose _____

_____

3. Unscramble these questions. Remember to use question marks.

a. gold lost a Who watch _____

b. socks lying the are floor Whose on _____

c. book What you reading are _____

d. in with Who playing park the was you _____

e. is to river it Which way the _____

4. Fill in the missing pronouns in these sentences.

a. _____ is Dad doing in the shed?

b. _____ was that masked man?

c. _____ flavor do you like best, chocolate or vanilla?

d. _____ dog is that running down the street?

e. To _____ it may concern . . .

Assessment - Pronouns

CHECK 1: Are the underlined words pronouns? Write "Yes" or "No." ☐ /5

   a. Do you know if the doll is <u>hers</u>? _____

   b. The kitten cut its paw <u>on</u> the wire. _____

   c. Stand up and let me look at <u>you</u>. _____

   d. Butter <u>some</u> toast for breakfast, please. _____

   e. <u>It</u> looks very stormy in the west. _____

CHECK 2: Circle the pronouns in these sentences. ☐ /10

   a. The children went to see a movie. They all enjoyed it very much.

   b. After school, Thomas goes to see his friend. They play computer games.

   c. Pam took her ballet slippers out of their box.

   d. Did you want to come and play with us?

   e. Saul enjoyed reading the book that I gave him.

CHECK 3: Fill in the spaces with suitable pronouns. ☐ /12

   a. Wait for _____, please.

   b. _____ gave _____ sister a box of chocolates.

   c. Will _____ come to the park with _____?

   d. Paul gave _____ the book because _____ had finished reading _____.

   e. Will _____ go to school together today?

   f. The boys lined up. The coach told _____ that _____ was happy with _____ game.

CHECK 4: Use arrows to show which nouns were replaced by pronouns. ☐ /8

    a. Joe can't carry the bucket, because it is too heavy.

    b. Theo and Jade like books. They read every day.

    c. Rob visited his Aunt Sue. He gave her a rose.

    d. Mrs. Wong nodded. The boys gave their books to her.

    e. "Do you want to come with me?" Rani asked Chloe.

CHECK 5: A pronoun is missing from each sentence. Mark the spot with a ^ and write what the pronoun is. ☐ /5

    a. He put hand under his chin. _____

    b. Do always put your toys away? _____

    c. With their blocks made a tall tower. _____

    d. That is his hat. Give back to him. _____

    e. Will you come and see after school? _____

CHECK 6: Underline only the pronouns that are used instead of "Sally." ☐ /10

Sally looked up and she could see the beach.

Mr. Green could see why she was sad. Two big tears rolled down her cheeks.

"Sally," he said, "I am not going to keep you. You are free to go. You will be happy here."

Sally held up her flipper, and Mr. Green gave it a squeeze. Then she went down to the sea.

She waved her flipper and dived into the waves.

Student Name: _____

Date: _____

Total Score: _____/50

PRONOUNS

VERBS

Verbs consist of one or more words that show the particular interactions and relationships between people, place, events, and objects.

Verbs are the essential ingredient of any sentence. Without them, communication is, at best, poor. A verb gives a sentence a reason for "being." It informs of some process occurring between people and things. In the fast growing world of telecommunications, new language is being created all the time. New verbs are being born, while others are being discarded or archived. We now have, for example, the verbs *email, text, merge, autoformat*, etc.

Verbs tie ideas together and make sense of them. They contextualize the events surrounding people, places, and things. Verbs are very powerful tools used by writers and speakers. Writers, especially, recognize the power in verbs to create strong images of movement, action, and behavior. Like adjectives, verbs give color and interest to sentences. They create vivid pictures of motion and movement, so they can be used to great effect, especially in descriptive writing and poetry.

Help students create a verb-consciousness to build a vocabulary that is colorful and imaginative. Help them leave words like "got" behind and strive for words of color, precision, and expression.

Different verbs have different jobs to do.

"Doing" verbs show the actions of people and things.

e.g., fly, swim, sleep, break, spill, dance, cry, wrap

"Being" verbs show that people and things exist.

e.g., am, is, are, was, were, be, being, been

"Having" verbs show what people and things "have."

e.g., has, have, having, had

"Saying" verbs show how living things (or personified objects) express themselves.

e.g., growl, squeak, shout, whimper, howl, whisper, say, call, cry

"Thinking" verbs show how people mentally process ideas.

e.g., imagine, think, ponder, believe, visualize, reminisce, cogitate, remember

Verbs have different forms.

An **infinitive** is the simple verb form.

e.g., to play, to swim, to eat, to take

Finite verbs work on their own. They have someone or something as the subject.

e.g., *Golden autumn leaves* <u>fall</u> from the trees.
The jet plane <u>flew</u> to Melbourne.

Non-finite verbs cannot work on their own. They consist of the following:

1. infinitives (e.g., I want <u>to eat</u>. Jani wants <u>to play</u>.)

2. present or past participles with an auxiliary verb (e.g., She <u>is singing</u> on stage. He <u>was playing</u> hockey. Mom <u>has baked</u> a pot roast dinner. Ferris <u>had kicked</u> the winning goal.)

The **present participle** is formed by adding –*ing* to the infinitive.

e.g., fly, flying; jump, jumping

The **past participle** is formed by adding –*ed* to the infinitive.

e.g., kick, kicked; play, played

Auxillary (helping) verbs are used with present and past participles to make a complete verb. Their job is to show tense or possibility.

e.g., We <u>are eating</u> dinner. (present tense)
They <u>were eating</u> dinner. (past tense)
I <u>may go</u> to Sydney next week. (possibility)

A **singular verb** is used with a singular subject.

e.g., A dog chews bones.
A cat drinks milk.

A **plural verb** is used with a plural subject.

e.g., The dogs chew bones.
The cats drink milk.

Verbs show tense.

It is the verb in a sentence that determines when something occurs. Verbs indicate three different times, called *tenses*.

1. **present tense:** I <u>am playing</u> tennis.

2. **past tense:** Shane <u>played</u> soccer for America.

3. **future tense:** They <u>will play</u> the final match on Saturday.

Regular/Irregular Verbs

Most verbs show tense in a regular way through the use of present or past participles.

e.g., I am dancing. (present) I danced. (past)
    He is washing his car. (present)
    He washed his car. (past)

Irregular verbs change their spelling in the past tense and the past participle.

e.g., ring, rang, rung; do, did, done

Other examples of irregular verbs include *go, fly, eat, give, take, know.*

A **verb group** is a group of words built around a verb. They contain auxillary verbs, participles, or infinitives.

e.g., He <u>was sleeping</u> on the couch.
    Tom <u>wanted to go</u> early.
    I <u>have been living</u> here for six months.

These verb groups indicate the processes in text.

Contractions

We often contract verb and (pronoun) subject.

e.g., I am = I'm; it is = it's; they are = they're

We often contract verb and negative.

e.g., will not = won't; cannot = can't;
    did not = didn't

Homographs

Many words can do the work of both a noun and a verb.

e.g., Her head is steady as a <u>rock</u>. Don't <u>rock</u> the boat.

Their job is determined by the context. Other examples include *bear, paint, play, plan, block, post.*

Verb-forming suffix

Some verbs are easily identified by their suffixes (word endings).

e.g., oper<u>ate</u>, telev<u>ise</u>, light<u>en</u>, wait<u>ing</u>, tramp<u>ed</u>

Ideas for introducing verbs

- Ask the students to imagine they are magpies and write one word that says what they can do. Write a selection of these words (infinitives) on the board (e.g., fly, peck, warble, hop, eat).

- Repeat the process, asking the students to imagine they are athletes, dogs, cooks, or ants. List all their "doing" words on the board.

- Introduce the term *verb*, a word that says what people and things do.

- Write a subject on the board (e.g., spiders). With the students, make a list of all the things that spiders can do (e.g., crawl, climb, spin, leap, bite, wait).

- Ask the students to give you a sentence (orally) about spiders using a listed verb. Add it to the board and discuss.

- Now ask the students to give you a sentence beginning with "The spider . . ." Most students will offer a sentence where the verb has been formed by changing or adding to the infinitive (e.g., The spider is climbing up the wall. The spider waited to catch the fly. The spider spun its web.) This will give you the opportunity to speak about the verb in a sentence being one or more words and that verbs show when things happen.

- Write a sentence on the board and ask the students to identify the verb, the "doing" part of the sentence.

- Hand out a prepared text that illustrates only "doing" verbs, and ask the students to highlight the verbs.

- Ask them to list five "doing" verbs from a book they are reading. Share their lists and discuss whether the chosen words are verbs or not.

Exploring VERBS

A Tense Time

Divide the class into groups of four or five. Give each group a sheet of paper with three columns labeled "Present," "Past," and "Future."

Give each group a bundle of paper slips with verbs or verb groups written on them (e.g., jumps, was following, patted, will run). Ask the groups to discuss and decide where each verb should be placed. The slips are then glued onto the sheet. The groups present their chart to the class. Discuss any inaccuracies. Conclude with some generalizations, such as the following: past tense verbs most often end in –ed; helping verbs tell us whether a verb is past, present, or future.

Pet Patrol

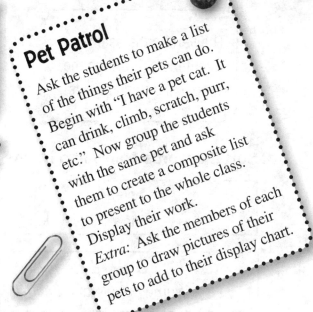

Ask the students to make a list of the things their pets can do. Begin with "I have a pet cat. It can drink, climb, scratch, purr, etc." Now group the students with the same pet and ask them to create a composite list to present to the whole class. Display their work.

Extra: Ask the members of each group to draw pictures of their pets to add to their display chart.

Keywords

Give each pair of students a magazine or calendar picture and a tagboard with two columns labeled "Nouns" and "Verbs."

Give them word cards containing nouns and verbs about the picture—about 10 of each. Ask the students to sort the words and place them in the correct column. Move among the students, observing and guiding their choices, if necessary. When complete, the materials could be stored in a plastic, zipper bag for reuse.

Extra: Ask the students to write one or two sentences about the picture using the nouns and verbs as keywords.

Mime Time

In small groups, students decide on a bird or animal they could pretend to be. Each member then decides on an action to mime to show what the creature can do. Each group should present their creature, one member at a time.

The class is to guess what the creature is and what it can do. The teacher may like to make a list (e.g., A bird can fly, peck, climb, walk, glide, etc.).

"Doing" Verbs 1

"Doing" verbs are the words that show what people and things are doing.

The verb is the heart of a sentence. It brings the people and things to life.

For example:

people

- talk
- sleep
- sit
- read
- drink
- eat

1. Sort the words below into nouns and verbs.

| horse | sun | eat | school | sing |
| mow | lose | fork | grow | chair |

NOUNS *Name people and things*	VERBS *Say what people and things are doing*

2. Some words can do the work of nouns and verbs. Can you say what the underlined words are? Use (n) for noun and (v) for verb.

a. I will <u>water</u> (   ) my new potted <u>plant</u> (   ).

b. Did you <u>sleep</u> (   ) well last night?

c. Ella went for a <u>swim</u> (   ), and I went for a <u>walk</u> (   ).

d. Katy had a <u>sandwich</u> (   ) for lunch.

e. Here is a can of <u>paint</u> (   ) to <u>paint</u> (   ) the fence.

3. Write two sentences using the word *wave*—first as a noun, then as a verb.

_____

_____

"Doing" Verbs 2

"Doing" verbs are the words that show what people and things are doing.

1. Select a verb from the list to match each noun.

a.	pigs	blows	*g.*	bees	gallop
b.	babies	ring	*h.*	birds	crawl
c.	rain	swim	*i.*	balls	bark
d.	fish	cry	*j.*	horses	fly
e.	wind	grunt	*k.*	dogs	buzz
f.	bells	falls	*l.*	ants	bounce

2. Put the "doing" verb in the space and draw one of your answers.

a. I _____ a model of a submarine.

b. _____ the gate behind you.

c. A truck _____ around the corner.

d. An old man _____ slowly by.

e. A green frog _____ onto the brown log.

3. Circle the verbs.

a. Wash your face and brush your teeth, Chen.

b. Tom took two apples but only ate one.

c. The horse bucked and the rider fell off.

d. Dad sold his old car and bought a new one.

e. I leaned out the window and lost my hat.

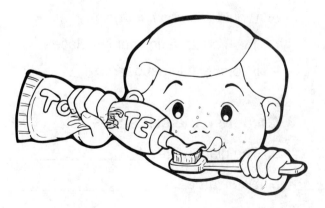

VERBS

"Saying" Verbs 1

Verbs can show how people express their feelings. We call this type of verbs **"saying" verbs**.

1. Choose a suitable word from the box to complete each sentence.

a. "Oh, a cockroach!" _____ Jill.

b. "Would you like another cup of tea?" _____ David.

c. "Shhh. It's a secret," Chandra _____.

d. "Are you coming?" _____ Jackson.

e. Lee _____, "That's really funny."

| asked |
| laughed |
| squealed |
| whispered |
| called |

2. Answer "yes" or "no." Use a dictionary, if necessary.

a. Would you *mumble* . . .

if you wanted everyone to hear you?   _____

if you were annoyed?   _____

b. Would you *complain* . . .

if you were treated unfairly?   _____

if you won first prize in a competition?   _____

c. Do young children *whine* . . .

when they are tired?   _____

on Christmas morning?   _____

d. Would you *grumble* . . .

if you got good grades in spelling?   _____

if your dad turned off the television?   _____

e. Would you *shout* for help . . .

if you couldn't tie your shoelaces?   _____

if you were in danger?   _____

3. Complete the sentences.

a. The giant roared, "_____."

b. Dad warned us _____.

c. "_____," someone shouted.

"Saying" Verbs 2

"Saying" verbs can show how people express their feelings. (Helen <u>cried</u>. Tammy <u>screeched</u>. Niko <u>shouted</u>. Harry <u>moaned</u>.)

1. Choose a suitable "saying" verb from the word list below to complete the sentences. Use a dictionary, if necessary. (NOTE: You may need to add *-ing* or *-ed*, so remember your spelling rules.)

a. "I can't hear you, Mrs. Jones," _____ Leanne.

b. Someone was _____ from the upstairs window.

c. "I've lost my new lunch box," Jai _____.

d. "You'll never find out what it is!" _____ Heather.

e. "Get out of my way," _____ the angry driver.

f. "You're late again," the teacher _____.

g. "What a wonderful surprise!" _____ Farida.

h. "You must never do that again," their mother _____.

i. "What a baby you are sometimes, Bobby," his sister _____.

j. Patrick _____, "I always get my answers right."

"Saying" Verbs Word List			
announce	gasp	nag	sneer
argue	giggle	prattle	snicker
ask	gossip	promise	sniffle
babble	growl	pray	snort
boast	grumble	rant	sob
blab	grunt	rave	sputter
brag	hit	roar	stammer
call	howl	say	stutter
chat	hum	scoff	talk
complain	jeer	scold	tease
cough	laugh	scream	tell
cry	moan	shout	wail
demand	mock	shrug	warn
drone	mumble	sigh	weep
exclaim	murmur	sing	whine
explain	mutter	smile	whisper

VERBS

"Being" and "Having" Verbs

The word "be" is used as a verb. The **"being" verbs** are as follows:

*am, is, are, was, were, *be, *being, *been*

Parts of the Verb "To Be"

am	I <u>am</u> ten years old.	**were**	The horses <u>were</u> restless.
is	George <u>is</u> my brother.	***be**	I <u>will be</u> home soon.
are	We <u>are</u> at school.	***being**	You <u>are being</u> silly.
was	Thomas <u>was</u> still in bed.	***been**	Someone <u>has been</u> here.

(NOTE: *be*, *being*, and *been* are only used with other verbs)

The words "has," "have," and "had" are also used as verbs. (Examples: Jill <u>has</u> a pet bird. I <u>had</u> breakfast early. They <u>have</u> new shoes.)

---

1. Complete the sentences using "being" or "having" verbs.

a. Max _____ a fat dog.

b. She _____ a new friend.

c. John _____ an ice cream.

d. The girl _____ red ribbons.

e. Only one book _____ on the table.

f. They _____ in the park.

g. We _____ not very late.

h. Oscar _____ on the swing.

i. I _____ only seven.

j. Somali _____ a new hobby.

2. Underline the verbs.

a. The soldier has a medal.

b. We each had six jelly beans.

c. She is five, and her sister is eight.

d. He is tall, but you are taller.

3. Circle the correct verb in these sentences.

a. The cat (is, was) scared of the storm last night.

b. That man was (being, been) quite rude.

c. I (was, am) so hungry at this moment.

d. Molly and I (has, have) chicken pox.

VERBS

"Helping" Verbs 1

Some verbs help other verbs do their work. Together, they make a verb group. **"Helping" verbs** tell us <u>when</u> something is happening.

> *am, is, are, was, were*
> *be, being, been*
> *do, did, does*
> *has, have, had*
> *shall, will*
> *can, may, might, must*
> *could, would, should*

Here are some examples:

Jessica <u>is</u> running to the bus.

The dog <u>has</u> eaten the bone.

I <u>will</u> be driving to Los Angeles tomorrow.

Dad <u>might</u> take us to the zoo.

1. Circle the verb group in each sentence.

a. The cat is licking its paws.

b. Billy has been to Florida with his family.

c. We can go swimming on Friday.

d. Zoe may be waiting for her friends at the gate.

e. I will be playing soccer for the school team on Saturday.

2. Complete the verb groups.

a. I am _____ my vegetable garden.

b. All the girls have been _____ caramel apples.

c. We were _____ in the tide pools by the shore.

d. A cow was _____ along the track.

e. They will be _____ to school soon.

3. Color only the helping verbs to spell out a word in the grid.

well	can	lost	has	jump	is
fly	was	see	am	come	shall
sleep	are	have	can	swim	may
run	will	read	do	look	had
eat	have	skate	might	sing	did

VERBS

"Helping" Verbs 2

A verb is sometimes separated from its helper by another word. (Examples: I <u>have</u> often <u>seen</u> him here. <u>Did</u> you <u>go</u> home early?)

1. Underline the verb group in each sentence. Do not underline words that are interrupting the verb.

a. It has just started to rain.

b. Have you read this book yet?

c. We will probably go by train.

d. He is always playing computer games.

e. Did they win the football game?

A verb can be made negative by placing "not" or "never" after the helper. (Examples: I do <u>not</u> want chips. They will <u>never</u> come back again. You are <u>not</u> to swim here.)

---

2. Complete these negative sentences.

a. I do not like _____.

b. Mom will not let me _____.

c. Liz does not _____.

d. The dog could not _____.

e. Kenji will not eat _____.

3. Rewrite the sentences in negative form.

a. We will play tennis on Saturday.

_____

b. The pig is in its pen.

_____

c. They have been to the rodeo.

_____

d. Wait for me!

_____

VERBS

Verbs – Contractions

Many negative verbs are written as **contractions**. (Examples: did not = didn't, is not = isn't, have not = haven't)

The helping verb and "not" contract into one word. An apostrophe replaces the "o" in "not."

1. Underline the contractions. Write the words they replace in the parentheses.

a. She said that she <u>wouldn't</u> come with me.   (_____would not_____)

b. The car hadn't been washed for weeks.   (_____)

c. Why didn't you shut the door?   (_____)

d. There weren't any chairs to sit on.   (_____)

e. It isn't raining yet.   (_____)

2. Match and color the contractions with the words they replace. Use different colors for each contraction.

a. doesn't	had not	*e.* didn't	would not	*i.* haven't	do not
b. won't	were not	*f.* wouldn't	was not	*j.* aren't	have not
c. hadn't	does not	*g.* can't	cannot	*k.* don't	could not
d. weren't	will not	*h.* wasn't	did not	*l.* couldn't	are not

3. Rewrite these sentences in negative form using contractions.

a. The dogs can hunt foxes.   _____

b. We will be going to the show.   _____

c. Have you seen that movie?   _____

d. The lawn has been mowed.   _____

4. Complete the sentences.

a. The sheep aren't _____ .

b. Won't you come _____ .

c. I just couldn't _____ .

VERBS

Verb - Subject Agreement

Simple sentences have two parts. The verb ties the subject to the rest of the sentence.

The old horse / lives on a farm near the coast.

Subject   Predicate

1. Put a box around the subject of each sentence. The verb is underlined.

a. The tired cat <u>is sleeping</u> on the soft rug.

b. My best friend <u>rides</u> a BMX bike.

c. Not far away <u>was</u> a large shopping center.

d. Jill <u>drank</u> a glass of sparkling lemonade.

e. At the corner of the street, the bus <u>stopped</u>.

A singular subject has a singular verb. A plural subject has a plural verb.

Example: <u>The old horse</u> lives on a farm.

<u>The old horses</u> live on a farm.

A verb should always agree with its subject.

2. Rewrite each sentence in its plural form.

a. The snake slides into the hollow log.

_____

b. A passenger is boarding the jet plane.

_____

c. The girl is in the tree house.

_____

d. A golden leaf was falling to the ground.

_____

e. In the night sky, the star is twinkling.

_____

VERBS

Verbs – Contractions

Many subjects and verbs are written as **contractions**. (Examples: she will = she'll; I would = I'd; we have = we've; they are = they're)
Usually, a pronoun subject and a helper verb contract to one word. (Example: he is = he's)

An apostrophe marks the spot!

1. Match and color the contractions with the words they replace. Use different colors for each contraction.

I'll	they have	I'm	it is	I've	we will
he's	you have	you're	we have	you'll	they would
they've	I will	they're	you are	he'd	you will
we're	she would	it's	he will	she's	I have
she'd	he is	he'll	they are	they'd	he would
you've	we are	we've	I am	we'll	she is

(NOTE: I <u>should've</u> come with you. should've = should have NOT should of)

2. Circle the contractions. Write the two words in full.

a. I know (they've) been here before (__they__ __have__)

b. It's wonderful to see you again. (_____ _____)

c. I'm sure that she'll come with us. (_____ _____) (_____ _____)

d. We're so pleased you've arrived. (_____ _____) (_____ _____)

e. I'd like to know why they're late. (_____ _____) (_____ _____)

f. You'll be happy that he's coming. (_____ _____) (_____ _____)

3. Circle the correct word in the pair.

a. (Your   You're) not afraid of the dark, are you?

b. (Were   We're) off to the beach for vacation.

c. (There   They're) too old to run fast.

d. I would love to see (its   it's) nest.

VERBS

Verbs - Tense

Verbs tell us <u>when</u> things are happening.

I <u>am running</u> to school.

I also <u>run</u> to school

I <u>ran</u> to school.

I <u>will run</u> to school soon.

PRESENT
is happening now

PAST
has happened

FUTURE
is going to happen

1. Write five things that are happening **NOW**.

The sun is shining.

a. _____

b. _____

c. _____

d. _____

e. _____

2. Complete these present-tense happenings and then draw them.

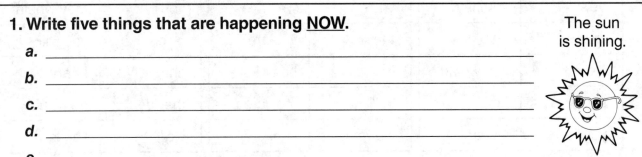

a. A bird ____ flying.	*b.* The balls ____ bouncing.	*c.* These dogs ____ barking.

3. Complete these sentences.

a. Last night, I _____. _____

b. Ten minutes ago, _____. _____

c. Yesterday morning, _____. _____

d. When I was a baby, _____. _____

Go back and circle all your verbs or verb groups. Write the tense here.

Verbs - Past Tense
Verbs tell us when things are happening.

1. Add a verb or verb group in the past tense.

> Many past tense verbs are formed by adding –ed. For example: jump—jumped; move—moved; hop—hopped (*Note:* Some words may already have an "e." If so, just add a "d." Some words may also have double consonants, such as *hopped*.)

a. The men _____ up into the mountains.

b. Jake _____ the ball to me.

c. The sails of the windmill _____ round and round.

d. Katy _____ her pet kitten.

e. The horse _____ across the pasture.

2. Write the past tense of these verbs.

a. help _____ **f.** share _____ **k.** plan _____

b. rain _____ **g.** close _____ **l.** step _____

c. cook _____ **h.** change _____ **m.** pin _____

d. stay _____ **i.** live _____ **n.** rob _____

e. want _____ **j.** invite _____ **o.** grin _____

Spelling alert! | Other verbs change their spelling in the past tense.

3. Write the past tense of these verbs.

a. eat _____ **e.** is _____ **i.** run _____

b. give _____ **f.** sing _____ **j.** has _____

c. come _____ **g.** grow _____ **k.** stand _____

d. dig _____ **h.** do _____ **l.** break _____

4. Change the present tense verb (underlined) to past tense.

a. We <u>buy</u> eggs. _____bought_____ **d.** They <u>sit</u> on chairs. _____

b. I <u>light</u> a candle. _____ **e.** She <u>sees</u> a cow. _____

c. He <u>runs</u> fast. _____ **f.** We <u>spend</u> money. _____

VERBS

Verbs – Future Tense

Verbs tell us when things are happening.

1. Write sentences to say what you think you will be doing.

a. tomorrow   *b.* next week   *c.* this evening   *d.* when you grow up

a. _____

b. _____

c. _____

d. _____

Go back and circle your verb groups. These verbs show future tense.

2. Draw a picture to complete the sentence.

a. I will eat that

b. We will buy some

3. Read the sentences below. On a separate sheet of paper, draw a table with columns labeled "Past," "Present," and "Future." Copy the sentences into the correct column.

a. He was upset when he lost his school hat.	*d.* I will brush my teeth after dinner.	*g.* The race driver drove his car at top speed.
b. Mrs. Singh is cooking a pot of soup.	*e.* Brett was chosen for the soccer team.	*h.* They are singing pop songs.
c. Dad will read the newspaper before he goes to work.	*f.* Alex will be talking to the class about the planet Mars.	*i.* I am writing an email to my uncle.

VERBS

Verbs – Suffixes 1

Some verbs have **suffixes** (word endings). (Examples: sep<u>ar</u><u>ate</u>, ope<u>rate</u>, leng<u>then</u>, gar<u>gle</u>, hudd<u>le</u>, adver<u>tise</u>, recog<u>nize</u>)

1. Complete the words in this tale by adding *–ing* or *–ed*. Watch your spelling.

One day, a beautiful cat was walk_____ near the palace of a king. She pride_____ herself on her fine looks and good manners. That morning, she was feel_____ very hungry. She was look_____ for something to eat. A bird hop_____ on the grass, and the cat snatch_____ it with her paw. The poor bird was frighten_____. "What are you go_____ to do with me?" ask_____ the bird, try_____ to think of a way to trick the cat.

2. All these verbs end in the suffix *–le*. Name something that . . .

a. would make you chuckle. _____

b. would make you tremble. _____

c. would sparkle in the sun. _____

d. you might dangle. _____

e. might make you stumble. _____

f. you could juggle. _____

g. might startle you. _____

3. Search out these verbs. They all end in the suffix *–en.*

lengthen

widen

flatten

weaken

stiffen

open

shorten

strengthen

B	W	S	L	G	U	K	R	T	P
S	T	R	E	N	G	T	H	E	N
H	I	F	N	C	C	D	L	M	E
O	R	D	G	A	B	J	U	N	T
R	O	S	T	I	F	F	E	N	T
T	H	Y	H	Z	H	T	F	C	A
E	O	P	E	N	D	W	X	K	L
N	M	I	N	S	R	U	A	H	F
N	E	D	I	W	E	A	K	E	N

VERBS

Verbs - Suffixes 2

Suffixes change the way words are used. The suffixes *–ize*, *–ate*, and *–ify* indicate verbs.

1. Match these verbs with their meanings.

a. minimize	to make use of
b. apologize	to find fault with
c. utilize	to remember something seen before
d. criticize	to make smaller
e. recognize	to say you're sorry

2. Use three of these verbs in sentences.

a. _____

b. _____

c. _____

3. Write the verb form of the word in parentheses, using the suffix *–ify*.

a. Did the thunderstorm _____ you? (terror)

b. Put your thumb up to _____ you are ready. (sign)

c. Did the teacher _____ your parents? (note)

d. The council will _____ our city parks. (beauty)

e. Could you _____ the thief? (identity)

4. Use the correct verb form from the list. Use a dictionary, if necessary.

a. The police will _____ the robbery.

b. Did the doctor need to _____ on her patient?

c. The machines will _____ the building site.

d. We will _____ Joel for team captain.

e. The farmer needs to _____ his cotton crop.

irrigate
operate
nominate
investigate
excavate

VERBS

Assessment - Verbs

CHECK 1: **Circle all the verbs or verb groups in this text.** ☐ /10

Brer Fox was angry that Brer Rabbit had tricked him so often. He decided that he would pay him back. He mixed some tar with turpentine and shaped it into a doll. He put a tall hat on its head. "This doll will catch Brer Rabbit," he thought and laughed.

CHECK 2: **Find the verb or verb group in each sentence.** ☐ /10
Circle the following:
   –verbs in past tense in <u>red</u>
   –verbs in present tense in <u>blue</u>
   –verbs in future tense in <u>green</u>.

a. At sunset the fishing boats will return to port.

b. Add a cup of flour to the mixture.

c. Doug waited at the bus stop for the bus.

d. The farmer is harvesting the wheat.

e. I will watch a new show on TV tonight.

f. Many houses were damaged in the storm.

g. Peter and his brother are playing marbles.

h. Kerry drove to the coast in her sports car.

i. We will enter the swimming competition.

j. Mr. Tan polished his car.

CHECK 3: **Are the underlined words nouns or verbs? Use (n) for noun and (v) for verb.** ☐ /10

a. <u>Turn</u> (   ) the volume down.

b. As a snake grows, it <u>sheds</u> (   ) its <u>skin</u> (   ).

c. This <u>watch</u> (   ) will not <u>work</u> (   ).

d. <u>Stick</u> (   ) a <u>stamp</u> (   ) on the envelope and <u>mail</u> (   ) it.

e. When we went for a <u>drive</u> (   ), we saw many street <u>signs</u> (   ).

VERBS

CHECK 4: Complete each sentence with a "saying" verb. ☐ /5

    a. "Ouch!" _____ Ben. "I've hit my finger again."

    b. "Shhh," _____ Tina, "you'll wake the baby."

    c. The angry man _____ at the truck driver.

    d. All the children _____ at his joke.

    e. I _____ to my best friend on the telephone.

CHECK 5: Write the contraction of the underlined words in the parentheses. ☐ /5

    a. We <u>could not</u> see the house in the fog.   (_____)

    b. <u>They are</u> playing outdoor games.   (_____)

    c. Mr. Jones said that <u>he would</u> soon be eighty.   (_____)

    d. <u>Can</u> you <u>not</u> see where you are going?   (_____)

    e. <u>You are</u> just in time for dinner.   (_____)

CHECK 6: Circle the correct verb. ☐ /5

    a. The plane (fly flies) high above the clouds.

    b. The street light (shine shines) on the wet streets.

    c. She (ride rides) her pony every day.

    d. Mr. Hopkins (live lives) at the corner of my street.

    e. My feet (is are) cold in the winter.

CHECK 7: Complete the verbs by adding –ing or –ed. ☐ /5

At the town carnival, Andrew saw the Ferris wheel go round and round. He saw children

rid_____ on merry-go-rounds and buy_____ popcorn and candy. But Andrew just want_____

to buy all the balloons he could hold. He found the balloon seller. He gave him his money and

ask_____ for all the balloons he could buy.

    The balloon seller sold him the whole big bunch of balloons. When Andrew took the balloons,

he float_____ up and up and up.

Student Name: _____

Date: _____   Total Score: _____/50

VERBS

ADVERBS

Adverbs are the words that add meaning to the actions of people, places, events, and objects. They tell us how, when, and where things happen.

While nouns give the things around us a name, adjectives give them a face, and verbs give them something to do or say.

Adverbs are the words that create the context of those actions.

They tell us about the movements, mood, mannerisms, and body language of the people or objects involved.

They tell us about the times and the places where events occur.

Adverbs add meaning to . . .

- a verb (e.g., He *runs* <u>fast</u>.)

- an adjective (e.g., He is a *very* <u>fast</u> runner.)

- another adverb (e.g., He runs *too* <u>fast</u> for me.)

Different adverbs have different jobs to do.

Adverbs of manner tell how something is done.

e.g., He nodded <u>anxiously</u>. She spoke <u>slowly</u>.

Many adverbs of manner end in *–ly*.

e.g., quickly, lazily, fiercely, silently, busily, angrily, warily

NOTE: A few words ending in *–ly* are adjectives.

e.g., early bird, curly hair

It is easy to spot the adverbs. They add meaning to verbs, adjectives, and other adverbs—never to nouns.

Adverbs of time tell when things happen.

e.g., yesterday, tomorrow, long ago, next week, on Tuesday, now

Adverbs of time also tell how often things happen.

e.g., often, seldom, usually, occasionally, once, twice, daily

Adverbs of place tell where things are happening.

e.g., here, there, everywhere, somewhere, away, around, over

Interrogative adverbs are used to ask certain questions.

e.g., <u>How</u> are you? <u>Where</u> did you come from? <u>Why</u> have you come? <u>When</u> will you go?

Negative adverbs are used to make sentences negative.

e.g., I do <u>not</u> agree.
They have <u>not</u> come yet.

In speech and informal writing, they are often written as contractions.

e.g., I do<u>n't</u> agree.
They have<u>n't</u> come yet.

Affirmative adverbs give the sentence a positive feel.

e.g., yes, certainly, undoubtedly, surely

Modal adverbs add a sense of possibility.

e.g., We <u>probably</u> will go.
She <u>possibly</u> won't.
<u>Perhaps</u> you will.

Adverbs of degree show the extent to which something happens.

e.g., very, almost, nearly, scarcely, completely, absolutely

Adverbs, like adjectives, also have three forms:

- positive degree
e.g., He shouted loudly.

- comparative degree
e.g., He shouted more loudly still.

- superlative degree
e.g., He shouted most loudly of all.

Generally, we add *–er* or *–est* to adverbs of one syllable.

e.g., high, higher, highest; hard, harder, hardest

Thus, some adverbs of degree will look like adjectives. Always remember that adverbs add meaning to verbs, adjectives, and other adverbs—never to nouns.

Adverbs ending in *–ly* have "more" or "most" before them.

e.g., silently, more silently, most silently

Some adverbs of degree are irregular.

e.g., well, better, best; much, more, most; badly, worse, worst

Ideas for introducing adverbs

- Have a brainstorming session with the class. List as many verbs as you can to show how people can move in different ways.

  e.g., run   climb   dash   hurry

  hobble   jump   shuffle   jog

  sprint   hop   walk   limp

  roll   creep   plod   sit

  crawl   skate   drive   stroll

  somersault   slide   prance   stagger

- Select one and write a sentence around it—e.g., The boy runs.

- Ask the students to offer words that will tell <u>how</u> the boy is running. Write these words, one under the other after "runs." Then get different students to read the new sentences.

  e.g., The boy runs quickly.

                       slowly.

                       fast

                       steadily

                       awkwardly

- Introduce the word "adverb"—a word we use to tell us how the boy is running.

- Repeat this process with a different sentence—e.g., The woman <u>drives</u>.

- Ask the students to choose a word from the list and write a short sentence, adding an adverb of manner.

- Write a number of these sentences on the board for discussion and comment.

- Together, write a definition of an adverb: *Adverbs tell us how something happens.*

- Go back to the original sentence, and this time, ask the students to say <u>when</u> the boy might run. Write their responses on the board. The sentence will change tense with different suggestions.

  e.g., The boy ran <u>yesterday</u>. The boy will run <u>tomorrow</u>. The boy runs <u>often/sometimes</u>.

- Again introduce the word "adverb"—a word we use to tell us when the boy is running.

- Again ask the students to choose a word from the list and write a sentence, adding an adverb of <u>time</u>.

- Write a number of these sentences on the board for discussion and comment.

- Add to your definition of an adverb: *Adverbs tell us how and when something happens.*

- Explain that adverbs also tell us <u>where</u> something happens. Illustrate with sentences like the following:

  e.g., The boy runs <u>backwards</u>. The boy runs away. The boy runs <u>here</u> and <u>there</u>.

- Add the final part of your definition: *Adverbs tell how, when, and where something happens.*

Exploring ADVERBS

Adverb Exchange

Prepare a number of "simple sentence" strips. You will need about five per pair of students, with each sentence on a different-colored card. Each sentence should contain an adverb of manner.

e.g., The balloon burst loudly. He crept softly up the stairs. The child spoke sulkily. She opened the box excitedly. The witch cackled wickedly.

Cut the sentences up, word-by-word, and store each of them in a small, plastic, zipper bag. Give each pair a small bag. Ask them to assemble and read their sentences. Then ask them to exchange one adverb for another and read the new sentence. Ask them to write down the silliest sentence they can make for sharing with the class (e.g., The witch burst softly yesterday.) Then return the words to the bag for reuse.

Howzat!

Divide the class into small groups, each with a sheet of paper, black markers, and a bundle of children's books. Ask one student from each group to write "How?" on the top of his or her paper. The groups' task is to find and list as many adverbs ending in –ly as they can from the book they have. Before they begin, demonstrate how to scan text and set a time limit for the task. When they have finished, give each group time to present and display its list. Discuss and reinforce that adverbs say how things happen.

This 'n' That

Prepare a list of about ten adjectives down the side of a sheet of paper (one per group). The adjectives should be ones that the students can convert to adverbs by adding –ly.

Here are some ideas: angry, careful, careless, dangerous, reckless, slow, quick, cruel, foolish, nervous, rude, strong, happy, unusual, kind, tender, noisy, greedy, clear, clean, quiet, soft, simple, cold.

Tell the students their job is to change the adjectives to adverbs by adding –ly. Before starting, review the spelling rule for words ending in "y." When the groups have completed their lists, share and discuss. Reinforce that adjectives add meaning to nouns, and adverbs add meaning to verbs.

Spin an Adverb Web

Prepare a number of papers with a sentence starter in the center of each.

e.g., Jack walked . . . , Sue danced . . . , Boys played . . . , The man drove . . . , Ants move . . .

Divide the class into groups of three or four and give each group one of the starters and a black marker. First, demonstrate how to "spin" a web of adverbs around a starter on the blackboard. Include adverbs that tell how, when, and where. Allow students time to spin their webs, then share.

Adverbs - Manner, Time, Place 1

An **adverb** is a word that tells us more about the verb. (Examples: The cat purrs <u>loudly</u>. The man shouted <u>angrily</u>. Wait <u>here</u> for me. Let's go play <u>now</u>.)

HOW?

The plane flew <u>quickly</u>.
Joe is climbing <u>slowly</u>.

WHEN?

The plane flew <u>yesterday</u>.
Joe is climbing <u>now</u>.

WHERE?

The plane flew <u>high</u>.
Joe is climbing <u>down</u>.

1. The adverb in each sentence is underlined. Does it say "how," "when," or "where" about the verb?

   a. Jason swam <u>slowly</u> to the edge of the pool. _____

   b. We will eat dinner <u>soon</u>. _____

   c. The yellow kite is flying <u>high</u>. _____

   d. We <u>often</u> go shopping. _____

   e. <u>Away</u> ran the mouse. _____

2. Circle the adverbs in each sentence. Remember adverbs tell "how," "when," and "where."

   a. We cheered loudly for our team.

   b. Ari is leaving early.

   c. Please wait quietly by the door.

   d. Your book is there on the table.

   e. You go now and I'll come later.

   f. She spoke softly so no one heard her.

3. Use these adverbs in sentences: *somewhere, afterwards, politely.*

_____

_____

_____

ADVERBS

Adverbs - Manner, Time, Place 2

An **adverb** is a word that tells us more about the verb. Adverbs tell us <u>how</u>, <u>when</u>, and <u>where</u> something happens.

1. Circle all the adverbs below. Then on the line write (H) for "how, (W) for "when," or (WH) for "where."

a. We are going away for a vacation. _____	**c.** Charlie easily swam the length of the pool. _____	**e.** The puppies slurped their food noisily. _____
b. The fish swam around the tank. _____	**d.** We often go to the creek for a picnic. _____	**f.** Our newspaper is printed daily. _____

2. Add an adverb to each sentence. The words in the box will help you.

a. The boy spoke _____. (how?)

b. _____ I went to a barbeque. (when?)

c. Bert is sitting _____. (where?)

d. _____, the old man stood up. (how?)

e. The swimmer dived _____ into the pool. (how?)

f. He _____ goes to concerts. (when?)

here	there
backwards	quietly
yesterday	wearily
often	quickly
sometimes	
once	

3. The adverbs have been underlined. Draw an arrow from the adverb to the verb that it tells more about. Do the adverbs tell "how," "when," or "where" about the verb?

a. David called <u>excitedly</u> to his friends. _____ how _____

b. I <u>often</u> watch football matches on television. _____

c. Jeremy tied the rope <u>carelessly</u>. _____

d. Sit <u>here</u> and work <u>quietly</u>. _____

e. The horse galloped <u>down</u> to the gate. _____

4. Circle the correct adverb.

a. Cars should be driven (dangerously   carefully   recklessly).

b. You should wait (softly   patiently   anxiously).

c. You should always speak (rudely   nervously   clearly).

d. Pet animals should be treated (kindly   cruelly   foolishly).

ADVERBS

Adverbs

Many **adverbs** are formed by adding –ly to the adjective. (Examples: slow—slow<u>ly</u>, brave–brave<u>ly</u>, smooth–smooth<u>ly</u>, cold—col<u>dly</u>)

1. **Complete the sentences by using adverbs. Make the adverbs by adding –ly to an adjective in the box.**

   Spelling alert!

proud
silent
dangerous
gentle*
heavy*

   a. The car swerved _____ around the corner.

   b. The old man leaned _____ on his walking stick.

   c. _____ the moon slips across the sky.

   d. The boat rocked _____ on the water.

   e. Mrs. Poulos looked _____ at her son.

2. **Circle the correct word in the parentheses.**

   a. Never treat animals (bad badly).

   b. (Careful Carefully), he took the hot cake from the oven.

   c. The children rushed (noisy noisily) out to play.

   d. She spoke (kind kindly) to her brother.

   e. Sit (quiet quietly) beside your mother.

3. **Join the sentence parts correctly.**

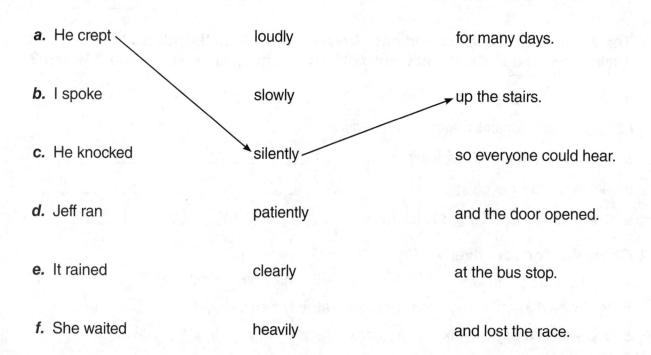

   a. He crept   loudly   for many days.

   b. I spoke   slowly   up the stairs.

   c. He knocked   silently   so everyone could hear.

   d. Jeff ran   patiently   and the door opened.

   e. It rained   clearly   at the bus stop.

   f. She waited   heavily   and lost the race.

Adverbs - Antonyms

We can use **adverbs** to show actions in opposite ways. (Examples: Did she speak <u>softly</u> or <u>loudly</u>? Did he do it <u>carefully</u> or <u>carelessly</u>?)

Adverbs that give opposite points of view are called **antonyms**.

1. To complete each sentence, write an antonym for the adverb in parentheses.

   a. That man is driving _____. (dangerously)

   b. The captain spoke _____ to his team. (loudly)

   c. He _____ rides his bike to school. (never)

   d. Jay treats his pet dog _____. (unkindly)

   e. Chris arrived _____ for school yesterday. (late)

   f. She will mail the letter _____. (soon)

2. Search for the antonyms (opposites) of these adverbs.

Y	L	T	F	O	S	J	O	K	R
L	B	G	E	L	D	W	X	L	B
H	I	G	H	P	R	Q	I	H	D
G	A	N	V	O	A	U	V	E	L
U	B	A	C	K	W	A	R	D	S
O	E	Z	E	L	P	E	F	I	O
R	L	G	H	Q	U	T	M	S	U
D	O	S	L	O	W	L	Y	T	T
R	W	Y	L	T	E	I	U	Q	H

smoothly

noisily

north

downwards

low

loudly

above

forwards

quickly

3. Use these adverbs in sentences: *carefully, carelessly.*

_____

_____

ADVERBS

Adverbs - Interrogative

Some adverbs are used to ask questions:
How? When? Where? Why?
(Examples: <u>Why</u> are you crying? <u>How</u> do you play chess? <u>When</u> are you going to Los Angeles? <u>Where</u> did I leave my shoes?)

1. Choose the correct adverb to complete these questions.

a. _____ will I find a book about boats?

b. _____ is she standing at the gate?

c. _____ do you make chocolate cookies?

d. _____ will the plane arrive from New York?

e. _____ must you leave so soon?

f. _____ far is it to Albert Park?

2. Answer these questions.

a. When is your birthday? _____

b. How old will you be? _____

c. Where do you live? _____

d. How far is your school from your home? _____

e. When do you get home from school? _____

f. Where do you play with your friends? _____

3. Unscramble these questions. Remember to use question marks.

a. the Why are laughing children

_____

b. is football the When final game

_____

c. plane make you How paper do a

_____

d. can Where comic I a buy book

_____

ADVERBS

Assessment - Adverbs

CHECK 1: The adverbs have been underlined. Do they say "how," "when," or "where" about the verbs?   ☐ /6

   a. Mary laughed <u>happily</u>.   _____

   b. <u>Soon</u> we will be going fishing.   _____

   c. The helicopter spun <u>sideways</u>.   _____

   d. Perhaps we could go bowling <u>tomorrow</u>. _____

   e. I am going <u>inside</u> for dinner.   _____

   f. Tiptoe as <u>quietly</u> as you can.   _____

CHECK 2: Circle the ten adverbs in this story.   ☐ /10

    Once the forest animals had a meeting. Kanga Kangaroo was in charge. He spoke quickly and excitedly. Wobbly Wombat walked into the meeting. He looked anxiously at Kanga. At the end of the table was Freddy Fox, waving his tail impatiently.

    "Friend, you are always late," said Kanga crossly.

    Wobbly mumbled something. "Speak properly," bellowed Freddy Fox loudly.

CHECK 3: Change these adjectives to adverbs.   ☐ /8

   a. lazy   _____   *e.* busy   _____

   b. steep   _____   *f.* strong _____

   c. wild   _____   *g.* thick   _____

   d. tidy   _____   *h.* rough _____

CHECK 4: Complete these questions that you might ask a famous person.   ☐ /4

   a. When _____?

   b. How _____?

   c. Where _____?

   d. Why _____?

ADVERBS

Assessment - Adverbs

CHECK 5: The adverbs have been underlined. Draw an arrow from the adverb to the verb it tells more about. ☐ /6

   a. The sails of the windmill turn <u>lazily</u> in the breeze.

   b. <u>Sometimes</u> I make chocolate fudge.

   c. He turned the bucket <u>upside down</u>.

   d. The family is strolling <u>slowly</u> along the beach.

   e. <u>Now</u> it is raining <u>heavily</u>.

CHECK 6: Write the antonyms (opposites) of these adverbs. ☐ /6

   a. early _____

   b. never _____

   c. inside _____

   d. roughly _____

   e. slowly _____

   f. carefully _____

CHECK 7: Circle the correct word in the parentheses. ☐ /5

   a. Our coach treats us (fair   fairly).

   b. The teacher nodded (wise   wisely).

   c. My sister walks too (slow   slowly).

   d. I am too (busy   busily) to speak.

   e. Be (quiet   quietly) while you wait.

CHECK 8: Join the sentence parts correctly. ☐ /5

   a. Come   away   and hurt her knee.

   b. She fell   brightly   over the rough road.

   c. The horse galloped   outside   in the blue sky.

   d. The truck bumped   heavily   and play with me.

   e. The sun shone   noisily   across the sandy hill.

Student Name: _____

Date: _____

Total Score: _____/50

Prefixes 1

A **prefix** is a word part added to the beginning of a word. It changes the meaning of the word. (Examples: <u>bi</u>cycle, <u>re</u>cycle, <u>tri</u>cycle; <u>up</u>scale, <u>down</u>scale, <u>super</u>market)

Prefixes *un-, in-, im-, dis-* = not, opposite of

1. Add one of these prefixes to change the meaning of the words: *un–, in–, im–, dis–*.
Use the dictionary, if necessary.

a. The red truck _____appeared around the corner.

b. I think that tale is _____true.

c. We all know that the teacher is very _____patient.

d. Your answer is _____accurate.

e. The final result is _____decided.

f. Did everyone _____agree with your plan?

g. Her behavior is quite _____appropriate.

h. It would be _____possible to get that job done today.

2. Make two new words by adding the prefixes.

	up–	*down–*
a. stairs		
b. stream		
c. hill		
d. right		
e. grade		
	over–	*under–*
f. weight		
g. take		
h. rate		
i. estimate		
j. sized		

PREFIXES

Prefixes 2

A **prefix** is a word part added to the beginning of a word. Some words can have several different prefixes, forming new words with very different meanings. (Examples: <u>dis</u>cover, <u>re</u>cover, <u>un</u>cover; <u>down</u>play, <u>re</u>play, <u>dis</u>play)

1. Circle the correct word in parentheses.

   a. The explorer (uncovered, discovered) a swift-flowing river.

   b. The newspaper keeps everybody (deformed, informed).

   c. A (triangle, rectangle) has four sides.

   d. The concert was (underway, subway) by 7:30.

   e. The block of wood was soon (converted, diverted) into a work of art.

   f. After repairs, the electrician (disconnected, reconnected) the power supply.

2. Write the correct word from the box below into each sentence.

   a. The cowboy will gather his cattle this _____.

   b. I usually buy _____ meat.

   c. Dinosaurs were _____ creatures.

   d. Did the weather report _____ a thunderstorm?

   e. The earthquake was followed by many _____.

   f. We bought Uncle Ken a bottle of _____ for his birthday.

prehistoric	aftershave	preposition	aftershocks
prepackaged	afterthought	afternoon	predict

A Note to the Teacher

PREPOSITIONS & PHRASES

Prepositions are little words whose job is to tell us about the position of someone or something. A phrase is a group of words without a verb or subject, often beginning with a preposition.

Now we come to prepositions, a wonderful bundle of bread-and-butter words that mean almost nothing on their own but have the important job of positioning people and objects in space.

They often stand at the front of a group of words called a *phrase*, and they give language its rhythmical flair. Read the example below.

Jack and Jill went out their back door, up the hill, and over the top, down the lane, into the park, up the tree, over the fence, into the barn, among the cows, through the pasture, in front of the fence, behind the gate, and sat under the apple tree.

Phrases, having no verb or subject, only make sense within a sentence, never on their own. However, the reader would get little information without the use of phrases.

A **preposition** introduces a phrase, which is a group of words containing a noun or pronoun, but no verb.

e.g., My hand could be . . .
> on the table, above the table, under the table, beside the table, over the table, below the table, behind the table, on top of the table, etc.

Other examples include the following:
for Edward, to her, among the chickens, until tomorrow.

Phrases add meaning and detail to sentences.

e.g., They are walking in the park.
> They are walking along the beach.
> They are walking to get some fresh air.

Different phrases have different jobs to do.

Prepositional phrases begin with a preposition.

- e.g., into the park, over the road, beside the creek, under the bridge, up the ladder, around the bend

Adjectival phrases do the same work as adjectives. They can begin with:

- a preposition
  e.g., A boy with red hair walked past the window.

- a present participle
  e.g., The diver, wearing a wet suit, slipped into the sea.

- a past participle
  e.g., We found a kitten abandoned in the street.

- an infinitive
  e.g., I got a message to wait here.

Noun phrases do the same work as nouns.

> e.g., Walking every day is good exercise. I like climbing trees.

Adverbial phrases do the same work as adverbs. There are four types of adverbial phrase:

- Time (when)
  e.g., I meet my friends after school.
  On weekends, we like to go fishing.

- Place (where)
  e.g., Put the box on the table.
  The cat is under my chair.

- Manner (how)
  e.g., He pushed with all his strength.
  She waited with great patience.

- Reason (why)
  e.g., The game was stopped because of rain.
  They worked hard to earn some money.

Ideas for introducing prepositions and phrases

- Write a short sentence starter on the board. e.g., The man drove . . .

- Ask the students to give you some words to add that could tell you where he drove. They will probably respond with phrases. Write these in a list and select students to read the created sentences.

  e.g, The man drove down the street.
  along the road.
  to Los Angeles.
  under a bridge.

- Introduce the word "phrase," *a group of words with no verb*. Explain that the work of these phrases is to say <u>where</u> the man drove.

- Rewrite the sentence and add a phrase such as "at high speed." Explain that this tells us how the man drove. Ask them to give you some more examples (e.g., at top speed, in a dangerous manner, below/above the speed limit).

- Again talk about what a phrase is. Explain that the work of these phrases is to say <u>how</u> the man drove.

- Now ask the students to add a phrase that says <u>when</u> the man drove. Write their answers (e.g., last week, on Friday, all through the night). Select students to read the newly created sentences.

- Explain that the work of these phrases is to say <u>when</u> the man drove.

- Restate that *a phrase is a group of words with no verb*. Tell the students that phrases can do the same work as adjectives, adverbs, and nouns. (Introduce adjectival and noun phrases in later lessons.) Tell them that without phrases, you often don't get enough information. Illustrate with the beginning example and the sentences the students created by adding phrases.

- Write one phrase on the board (e.g., over the hill).

- Explain that the first word in a phrase is very often a *preposition*. This is a word that puts people and things in certain positions (e.g., <u>up</u> the ladder, <u>down</u> the ladder). Ask what makes the two phrases different. Try some others (e.g., in the box, beside the box, over the gate, under the gate).

- Go back and ask the students to pick out the prepositions in the earlier phrases and circle them.

- Have a list of commonly used prepositions prepared. Display and ask students, orally, to think of a phrase beginning with a preposition from the list.

- Ask the students to write a phrase beginning with a preposition. Then ask them to use their phrase in a sentence. Take time to share and discuss their responses.

PREPOSITIONS

about	at	down	of	to
aboard	before	during	off	towards
above	behind	except	on	under
across	below	for	over	until
after	beneath	from	past	up
against	beside	in	since	upon
along	between	into	through	with
among	by	near	till	without
around				

Exploring PREPOSITIONS & PHRASES

On Your Feet!

Give each student one or two word cards containing a phrase (e.g., to the bus, up the tree, across the road, with a broken leg, from home).

Write a short sentence starter on the board, such as "The man walked. . . ." Tell the students you are looking for a phrase that would make sense when added to the end of the sentence.

Ask those students whose phrases would make sense to stand up. Allow all who stand up to respond. Ask the class to judge whether the sentences make sense or not. Discuss any inaccuracies.

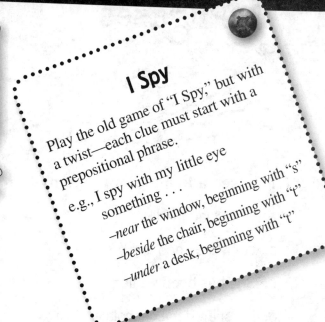

I Spy

Play the old game of "I Spy," but with a twist—each clue must start with a prepositional phrase.

e.g., I spy with my little eye something . . .

–near the window, beginning with "s"

–beside the chair, beginning with "t"

–under a desk, beginning with "t"

Sevens *(for a group of 6)*

You will need 42 word cards of playing-card size. Prepare seven sets of six words in the following way: Write all the words in the list, one word per card. (Write numbers on the back of the cards so they can be easily sorted after use.)

1	2	3	4	5	6	7
into	bus	A	mouse	fat	a	marched
from	tent	The	magpie	large	a	scurried
outside	boat	The	monster	young	the	stepped
behind	house	One	dragon	clever	the	crept
towards	train	This	ghost	cheeky	this	shuffled
through	caravan	That	robot	friendly	that	waltzed

Stack each set of words next to the others (seven piles). Ask each member of the group to take one card from each pile (seven words each). Ask them to arrange their words into a sentence. When they have done that, ask them to take turns reading their sentences to each other. This should create some laughter! The cards are returned to their correct pile, and play starts again.

Extra: Ask the students in the group to write down their last sentence to share with the class.

Prepositions & Phrases

A **phrase** is a group of words within a sentence without a verb. (Examples: out the door, up the tree, into our cubby, off to school.)

A phrase has no verb. It adds important information to a sentence.

1. Phrases add important information. Join these phrases so they make sense.

a. We all laughed   for you.

b. I only took one apple   under a tree.

c. She has been waiting   with me.

d. He shared the chocolate   at the clown.

e. The tired farmer sat   from the bowl.

2. Draw what is missing. The phrases will help you know what to do.

A frog is sitting <u>on a log</u>.	I am standing <u>under an umbrella</u>.	Dad went <u>up the ladder</u>.
The cup fell <u>off the table</u>.	A duck walks <u>towards the lake</u>.	There's a dog <u>beside the chair</u>.

3. Circle the phrases.

a. The kitten hid under the rocking chair.

b. At home, we often play board games.

c. The clock on the wall has stopped ticking.

d. A big band marched down the street.

e. We saw the full moon in the sky.

f. Our car in the garage has a flat tire.

g. The runners jogged around the lake.

Prepositions

Prepositions are little words whose job it is to tell us about the position of someone or something. (Examples: <u>across</u> the road, <u>before</u> the party, <u>up</u> in space, <u>under</u> my bed)

about	behind	from	through
above	below	in	till
across	beneath	into	to
after	beside	near	towards
against	between	of	under
along	by	off	until
among	down	on	up
around	during	over	upon
at	except	past	with
before	for	since	without

1. Write some phrases beginning with different prepositions.

_____

_____

_____

_____

_____

2. Choose a preposition to fill the gaps.

a. Wipe the glasses _____ a soft cloth.

b. Wait _____ the door, please.

c. The dog went _____ the gate.

d. Children are playing _____ the beach.

e. We learn spelling _____ school.

f. Did you look _____ the shed?

g. Ants are crawling _____ the post.

h. The ball bounced _____ the table.

i. A snake slithered _____ a log.

3. Rewrite the sentences, changing <u>only</u> the preposition.

a. A cat sat by my chair. _____

b. He ran past the door. _____

c. She hurried towards the tree. _____

d. The truck went up the hill. _____

PREPOSITIONS & PHRASES

Adjectival Phrases

Adjectival phrases do the same work as adjectives. (Examples: the girl <u>with blue eyes</u>, the horse <u>in the pasture</u>, the cup <u>on the saucer</u>)

1. The adjectival phrases have been underlined. Circle the nouns they describe.

a. Please wash the cups <u>on the sink</u>.

b. He chose the chocolate <u>in the gold wrapper</u>.

c. The man <u>with sunburned skin</u> is a farmer.

d. Will you help me carry this box <u>of books</u>?

e. The bell <u>above the door</u> is made of brass.

2. Link the adjectival phrase to the noun it describes.

a. the curtains	in the jug
b. the vase	under the bed
c. the dog	over the window
d. the water	on the table
e. the cat	with the flea collar

3. Now use each noun and phrase from above in sentences of your own.

a. _____

b. _____

c. _____

d. _____

e. _____

PREPOSITIONS & PHRASES

Adverbial Phrases

Adverbial phrases do the same work as adverbs. (Examples: He ran <u>across the road</u>. Wait <u>until Friday</u>. He walked <u>with long strides</u>.)

They tell us <u>how</u>, <u>when</u>, <u>where</u>, and <u>why</u> about the verb.

1. Do the adverbial phrases say "how," "when," "where," or "why"?

a. <u>Before school</u>, we have singing practice. _____

b. Lean your bike <u>against the wall</u>. _____

c. He spoke <u>in a soft voice</u>. _____

d. Thank you <u>for your help</u>. _____

e. <u>In thirty seconds</u>, the alarm will ring. _____

f. The soldier was given a medal <u>for his bravery</u>. _____

2. Complete the sentences by choosing an adverbial phrase from the box.

into the pool	during the storm	in ten minutes
with a soft cloth	for your sister	on the stove
below the waves	after the party	under a log

a. He polished his shoes _____. *(how)*

b. The train will depart _____. *(when)*

c. _____ dived a spear fisherman. *(where)*

d. Take another apple _____. *(why)*

e. _____, branches broke like matchsticks. *(when)*

3. Write sentences using these adverbial phrases.

a. along the beach *b.* through the open window *c.* between the flags

a. _____

b. _____

c. _____

PREPOSITIONS & PHRASES

Assessment -
Prepositions & Phrases

CHECK 1: **Underline the phrases.** ☐ /10

On Saturday morning, we drove to the beach for the day. We had a picnic lunch in a park. In the afternoon, we went swimming in the surf. Dad and Craig played a game of mini golf. Elly and I paddled in the tide pools with Mom. We returned home in the late afternoon. It was good to get into bed.

CHECK 2: **Follow the instructions to draw the following.** ☐ /6

Put a boat on a lake.	Put a bird on top of a roof.	Put a dog beside a car.
Put a cow under a tree.	Put a spoon between two cups.	Put a kite up in a tree.

CHECK 3: **Build sentences around these phrases.** ☐ /4

a. without a hat	*c.* near the shed
b. during summer	*d.* against the fence

a. _____

b. _____

c. _____

d. _____

PREPOSITIONS
& PHRASES

CHECK 4: Do the adverbial phrases tell us "how," "when," "where," or "why"? ☐ /5

    a. Wild birds come to feed <u>in my back garden</u>.   _____

    b. <u>Every morning before school</u>, we run <u>around the track</u>.   _____ _____

    c. The man drove <u>at top speed</u> <u>to the hospital</u>.   _____ _____

    d. Take an apple <u>for lunch</u>.   _____

CHECK 5: Use an arrow to show which noun the adjectival phrase describes. ☐ /5

    a. A girl <u>in a red dress</u> was selling flowers.

    b. Will you have a cup <u>of coffee</u>?

    c. I saw a child <u>with a red balloon</u>.

    d. Everyone, <u>except Josh</u>, was playing baseball.

    e. All the people <u>with tickets</u> went into the game first.

CHECK 6: Join the sentence parts correctly. ☐ /5

a. The cowboy rode	at the ice rink	for a bone.
b. I borrowed a book	for the team	is such fun.
c. The dog waited	with great skill	from the library.
d. We all cheered	by the kitchen door	at the rodeo.
e. Skating	about China	who came first.

PREPOSITIONS & PHRASES

Assessment – Prepositions & Phrases

CHECK 7: Choose an adverbial phrase to complete each sentence. ☐ /5

for her dog	on the ladder	without a hat	in a loud voice
in the pasture	in the backyard	before winter	under the bridge

a. She whistled _____. *(why)*

b. _____, the farmer will plant his crop. *(when)*

c. The firefighter called out _____. *(how)*

d. _____, you'll see our tree house. *(where)*

e. Don't go _____. *(how)*

CHECK 8: Rewrite the sentences, changing only the prepositions. ☐ /5

a. The plane flew towards the city.

_____

b. He went up the ladder.

_____

c. Place a chair beside the table.

_____

d. We played a game with Ravi.

_____

e. Let's go jogging around the lake.

_____

CHECK 9: Do the phrases tell us "which" (adjectival) or "where" (adverbial)? ☐ /5

a. The horse by the gate belongs to Mr. Biggle. _____

b. Write your name on this page, please. _____

c. Can you see a man with a long, white beard? _____

d. She hung her shirt on a coat hanger. _____

e. The swimmer in the black cap won the race. _____

Student Name: _____

Date: _____ Total Score: _____/50

PREPOSITIONS & PHRASES

A Note to the Teacher

A sentence is a meaningful chunk of language. It contains a complete idea.

Sentences are the building blocks of our language, and it is through our spoken and written language that we understand each other and the world.

It is through language that we interact with each other, statement by statement, question by answer, request by response.

We have a vast array of words to choose from to enable us to give our utterances precise, unambiguous meaning.

We have a whole range of techniques that enable us to manipulate our language.

We can inspire and uplift our audience and move them to laughter or tears.

Language gives us the power to control the many situations that arise in our lives.

SENTENCES

A sentence is a chunk of language that must have at least one subject, one verb, and make sense. In written English, it is bound by a capital letter and a period, question, or exclamation mark.

A baby deer bounded across the snow.

When the curtain went up, everyone stopped talking.

Different sentences have different jobs to do.

Statements relate facts (or opinions) and are bound by a capital letter and a period.

e.g., He is entering college this year. There are thirty students in my class. Uniforms should be worn in all schools. Landing on the moon was the greatest event in history.

Questions ask for information and expect answers. They are bound by a capital letter and a question mark.

- They can begin with an interrogative adjective, adverb, or pronoun.
  e.g., Where did you find my keys? Whose are these? Which shirt do you like? Why didn't you wait?
- They can be written as a statement with a tag on the end.
  e.g., You will buy a ticket, won't you? They went swimming, didn't they?

Exclamations stress the importance of the emotion expressed in the sentence. They are bound by a capital letter and an exclamation mark.

e.g., What! You forgot your money! I'm going now, and I'm not coming back!

Commands request or demand an action from the listener or reader. They are bound by a capital letter and a period or exclamation mark. Commands usually begin with a verb in the present tense.

e.g., Cut out all the pictures on the page. Don't forget to bring a raincoat.

Switch on the light, please. Get out! And don't come back!

Sentences have three forms.

Simple sentences have two parts—a subject and a predicate, which contains the verb.

| *Little Bo-Peep* | *lost her sheep.* |

Compound sentences consist of two simple sentences joined by a comma and a coordinate conjunction—*and, but, so, yet, or, for, nor.*

e.g., Jake drove the car, and Mary read the map. I'd like to go to the football game, but I don't have a ticket. Jane is coming over, so we can play chess. Would you like to read, or do you want to play a game?

Complex sentences are made up of a main (principal) clause and one that depends on it (subordinate). The subordinate clause begins with a relative pronoun *(who, whom, which, that)* or a subordinate conjunction. Common conjunctions include the following: though, although, after, as, before, because, since, then, once, until, unless, where, wherever, when, whenever, while.

Punctuation of Sentences

Capital letters are used:

- for the first word in a sentence.
  e.g., There's a hole in my pocket.
- for proper nouns within sentences.
  e.g., She handed Mr. Jazz his ticket to New York.
- for the first spoken word in dialogue.
  e.g., Jim said, "My mom bought a rug at the market." His brother added, "And a little brown teapot."

• to emphasize words in a sentence
  e.g., You're SO bossy. You did WHAT?

Periods end statements and commands.
  e.g., The waterfall was spectacular. Close the
       gate.

Question marks end questions.
  e.g., I'm thirsty, aren't you? Do you want a can
       of cola?

Exclamation marks end exclamations.
  e.g., Trust Eddie to forget! What a surprise!

Commas are used:

• to separate words in a list.
  e.g., I bought apples, pears, bananas, figs, and
       watermelons.

• to separate a beginning phrase or clause from the
  rest of the sentence.
  e.g., Late that afternoon, we arrived home from
       our trip. Although we were tired, we
       unpacked the car.

• to separate an embedded phrase or clause from
  the rest of the sentence.
  e.g., Aunt Jean, wearing her purple hat, drove off
       to the shops. The storm, which we had been
       promised, did not materialize.

• to separate spoken from unspoken words in
  dialogue.
  e.g., "This is the house I once lived in," sighed
       Madison.

"It must have been fun," said Sue, "to sleep
up in that attic room."

Quotation marks are used around spoken words in
dialogue.
  e.g., "Dinner is at seven o'clock," called Mom.
       "What are we having?" Jo replied.

Apostrophes are used:

• with nouns to show possession (e.g., Jack's
  clothes)

• with contractions of pronouns and helping verbs
  (e.g., We've packed a picnic lunch. You're
  invited to come.)

• with contractions of helping verbs and negatives
  (e.g., I can't sleep. Ben didn't win. She wasn't
  lost.)

Sentences can be written from three different points
of view.

• *First-person point of view* is when a writer,
  speaker, or character is doing the "talking."
  e.g., I eat my greens.

• *Second-person point of view* is used when
  someone is spoken to or in imperative sentences.
  e.g., If you look, you will see your hat.
  e.g., Eat your veggies.

• *Third-person point of view* is used when writers
  and speakers talk about other people and things
  e.g., They were left behind with their teacher.

Ideas for introducing sentences

• Write a colorful verb on the board (e.g., crash).

• Ask the students what they think about when they
  see that word. Pick up on a topic from the answers
  that they give you and write it on the board (e.g.,
  truck).

• Ask them how we might say something about the
  truck and the crash. They will probably respond in
  sentences. Write some of these on the board:
  e.g., The truck crashed into a tree.
       The truck was going too fast and crashed.
       A truck and a car crashed.
       The truck crashed, and the driver was hurt.

• Tell the students that these are four ideas about a
  truck and a crash. Each idea is called a *sentence*.

• Repeat this process with another word (e.g., melt).
  Again talk about the concept of a sentence being

one idea. Point out that a sentence begins with a
capital letter and ends with a period. This "fences
in" the idea. We can tell where it starts and where it
ends.

• Write another colorful verb (e.g., squeeze) on the
  board. This time, list a number of topic words
  (oranges, hand, toothpaste, hole in the wall, etc.),
  and ask the students to pick one word and think of
  one idea for a sentence. Write several responses on
  the board.

• Ask the students for their understandings about a
  sentence.

• Write two more interesting verbs on the board, and
  ask students to write a sentence for each.

• Share, discuss, and reflect on their learning.

• Return to this process at a later date to extend their
  learning by introducing adjectives or adverbs.

Exploring SENTENCES

In the Bag

Cut out some captioned photos from a newspaper, about six to ten for every pair of students. Cut off the captions, and store the captions and photos in a plastic, zipper bag. Give each pair of students a bag and ask them to match the captions and photos. Ask them to take note of the number of sentences in a caption. Pairs should take turns to read the matched captions to each other. Discuss captions with the whole class. Captions and photos are then returned to their bag for reuse.

Variation: Give each student a newspaper photo to paste on a sheet of paper. Ask the students to draft and write a one-sentence caption underneath. Photo with captions could be presented and displayed.

Sentence Splits

Prepare some simple sentence strips, large enough for the students to handle easily. Cut the sentences between subject and predicate. Prepare about six sentences for every pair of students. Store in plastic, zipper bags.

Little Bo-Peep	has lost her sheep in the hills.
A wise owl	sat on a branch in the tree.

Give each pair of students a bag and ask them to join the sentences correctly.

When the sentences are assembled, the students should take turns reading them to each other. The sentence strips are then placed back in the bag and passed on to another pair or stored for reuse.

Photo Shoot

Take a series of digital photos of members of your class, classroom, school buildings, etc. Print the photos and give one to each student. Ask the students to prepare three sentences about the photo for publication. Photos and text can be collated into a class book, given a title, and shared with the class or with other classes.

Variation: Prepare the photos and text as a PowerPoint presentation and have a "showing." You might like to invite parents.

Sentences

A **sentence** is a group of words that house a complete idea. It is fenced in by a capital letter and a period. A sentence always makes sense.

We use sentences to talk to each other.

A sentence always has a verb.

1. Put a checkmark in the box next to the sentences.

a. over the hill ☐

b. He is eating fish and chips. ☐

c. the man in his truck ☐

d. Pass the salt. ☐

e. in our classroom ☐

f. The sun rose over the hills. ☐

g. Start the motor, please. ☐

h. waiting on the corner ☐

i. I can't play chess. ☐

j. Go away. ☐

2. Find the sentences. Put a box around them. Use a capital letter and a period.

My sister and I went walking in the park we saw a boy walking his dog and a girl on a red scooter my sister wanted an ice cream we found a stand and bought two big cones we sat under a big tree to eat them

3. Write one or two sentences around these ideas.

dive
_____
_____
_____

scurry
_____
_____
_____

SENTENCES

Sentences - Statements

Many sentences are **statements**. A statement begins with a capital letter and ends in a period. (Examples: I like apples. Dad fixed my bike. Mary sings pop songs. He has a pet lamb.)

1. Write a statement about each picture.

Sentences state facts or opinions.

> A <u>fact</u> is true.
> An <u>opinion</u> is what someone thinks is true.

2. Are these statements facts or opinions?

a. Sacramento is the capital of the California. _____

b. Most boys enjoy trail bike riding. _____

c. Drinking dirty water can make you sick. _____

d. The koala is Australia's favorite native animal. _____

e. Eating an apple a day will keep you healthy. _____

3. Write two facts and two opinions.

a. _____

b. _____

c. _____

d. _____

SENTENCES

Sentences - Questions

Many sentences ask **questions** and expect answers. A question begins with a capital letter and ends with a question mark. (Examples: What is your name? Do you watch TV? Why are you late?)

1. Answer the questions about these two pictures. Answer in sentences.

a. What is the family doing?

_____

b. How many people are on the bed?

_____

c. Who is helping the children?

_____

d. Where is the boy playing?

_____

_____

e. What is the boy doing?

_____

_____

f. What season do you think it is?

_____

_____

2. Here is a fun quiz for you to answer. Answer in sentences.

a. How many legs has a spider? _____

b. Where would find an oasis? _____

c. Why would you go to the theater? _____

d. Who would help sick people? _____

e. What is your favorite snack? _____

f. When would you see a rainbow? _____

©*Teacher Created Resources, Inc.*

SENTENCES

Sentences - Exclamations

Some sentences show sudden surprise, delight, or horror. They are called **exclamations**. An exclamation begins with a capital letter and ends in an exclamation mark. (Examples: Stop! Help! No way! What! Late again! Get out!)

1. Complete each sentence with a period or an exclamation mark.

a. I went to the pet shop to buy a white rabbit

b. The wallet was left on the bus

c. Man overboard

d. Let's play baseball in the backyard

e. What a wonderful party

2. Write an exclamation for each picture.

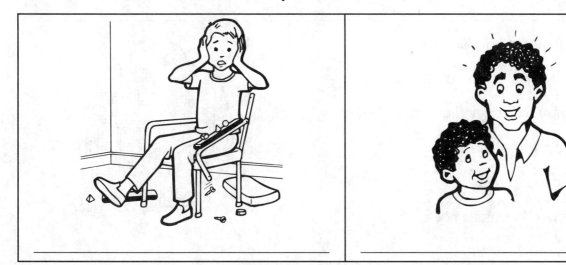

3. Draw a picture to match these exclamations.

Wow! Just what I wanted!

Everybody stand back!

SENTENCES

Sentences - Commands

Many sentences give **commands** and expect action. A comma begins with a capital letter and ends in a period. (Examples: Open the window gently. Add an egg into the mixture. Leave it on the table.)

Commands begin with a verb in the present tense.

1. Circle the verb in each command. What do you notice?

_____

a. Wear your plaid shirt, Bill.

b. Bake the scones in a hot oven.

c. Write your name and address here.

d. Stand at the end of the line.

e. Pass the pepper, please.

f. Bend the wire to make a hook.

2. Write your own commands. Begin with these verbs.

a. Sweep _____

b. Eat _____

c. Wait _____

d. Meet _____

e. Paint _____

f. Buy _____

SENTENCES

Sentences - Subject and Predicate 1

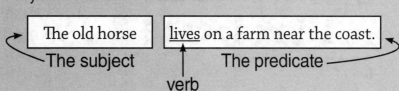

Simple sentences have two parts. One verb ties the subject to the rest of the sentence.

The old horse	<u>lives</u> on a farm near the coast.
The subject	The predicate

verb

1. **Put a box around the subject of each sentence. (TIP: Find the verb. Ask "who" or "what" does this?)**

   a. The hot air balloon floated high in the sky.

   b. A camel train crossed the sandy desert.

   c. Faster and faster, the go-cart rolled down the hill.

   d. My aunt sent me a birthday card.

   e. At the factory, tomato juice is bottled.

   f. Golden autumn leaves are falling from the trees.

2. **Write the correct subject for each sentence. Use the words in the box below.**

   a. _____ has a flat tire.

   b. At the supermarket, _____ bought jelly beans.

   c. _____ was born at the zoo.

   d. _____ handed in their test papers.

   e. Tires screeching, _____ sped around the corner.

   f. _____ is hanging on the doorknob.

my little sister	Your baseball cap	All the students
My red bike	the police car	A baby panda

©Teacher Created Resources, Inc.

#2435 Targeting Grammar

SENTENCES

Sentences - Subject and Predicate 2

Simple sentences have two parts. The subject is tied to the rest of the sentence, or predicate, by a verb.

1. Write four more sentences about the same subject.

<u>The old yellow bus</u> is traveling along the dusty road.

a. _____

b. _____

c. _____

d. _____

2. Add a subject so that each sentence makes sense.

a. _____ put three dollars in her piggy bank.

b. Up the steep hill went _____.

c. At the bottom of the hole, _____.

d. _____ escaped into the forest.

e. _____ lost his map and compass.

3. Write a predicate for each of these sentences that describe the picture.

a. The young man _____.

b. The sand castle _____.

c. The water _____.

d. A starfish _____.

SENTENCES

©*Teacher Created Resources, Inc.*

Compound Sentences

Two simple sentences, joined together, make a **compound sentence**. (Examples: I bought apples, <u>and</u> Jane bought figs. Tom likes pears, <u>but</u> his sister likes plums.)

Joining words are called **conjunctions**. Some joining words are *and*, *but*, and *so*.

1. Join the two sentences, using these conjunctions.

and	but	so

a. I am hungry, _____ I will eat lunch.

b. He wanted to go, _____ his dad wouldn't let him.

c. She called his name, _____ he didn't hear her.

d. Pia likes jelly beans, _____ she likes chocolate candy.

e. There's enough room in our car, _____ you can come with us.

2. Add your own sentence to make a compound sentence.

a. Jack played tennis, and _____.

b. I eat lettuce, but _____.

c. Saul wanted a pet bird, so _____.

3. Join two sentences with a conjunction by drawing lines.

a. Tom wants to go in the pool   and   you may go home.

b. Mia has black hair   the pool is full.

c. The bell has rung   so   I also like tea.

d. Greg knocked on the door   he can't swim.

e. I like coffee   but   Jacqui is blonde.

f. It rained heavily   no one answered.

SENTENCES

A word about CLAUSES

- A **clause** is a group of words with a subject and a verb.

  Examples: Dad and I went fishing.
  The athlete won a blue ribbon.

- A **principal clause** contains the main idea.
  A simple sentence has just one principal clause.

  Examples: Jayden likes watching action movies.
  Birds fly home at sunset.

- A **subordinate clause** says more about the main idea.
  It is linked to the principal clause by a joining word.

  Examples: I go swimming (principal) when the weather is hot (subordinate).
  I clean my teeth (principal) before I go to bed (subordinate).

- A subordinate clause is joined to the principal clause by a **conjunction** or a **relative pronoun**.

  Examples: She was late (principal) because (conjunction) she lost her way (subordinate).
  This is the house (principal) that (relative pronoun) Jack built (subordinate).

- These are the **relative pronouns** we use to join clauses:

  who, whom (used when talking about people)
  which, that (used when talking about things)

  These are the conjunctions we most often use to join clauses:

after	as	but	then	unless	whenever	while
although	because	once	therefore	until	where	
and	before	since	though	when	wherever	

 ©Teacher Created Resources, Inc.

Complex Sentences 1

A **complex sentence** is made up of a principal clause and a subordinate clause. They can be joined by a conjunction. (Examples: Put your scraps in the bin *when* <u>you have finished eating</u>.)

A subordinate clause can

be at the *beginning*, ⟶ <u>Before it gets too late</u>, I will catch a bus home.

in the *middle*, ⟶ The car, <u>because it is new</u>, is clean and shiny.

or at the *end* of a sentence. ⟶ The dams will be full <u>when the drought ends</u>.

---

1. Put a box around the principal clauses.

a. Kyle was unhappy because he had lost his football.

b. As we walked across the street, a car came rushing around the corner.

c. When you are ready, we will go to the skateboard park.

d. While I was at the beach, I collected a bucket of shells.

e. The audience went home after the concert was over.

2. Circle the subordinate clauses.

a. Did Mandy tell you where she was going?

b. We won't be in the final because we didn't win our last game.

c. Stand there until I tell you to move.

d. Although he is small, he is very strong.

e. I must get home before the sun goes down.

> A comma is needed after a subordinate clause <u>at the beginning</u> of a sentence.

3. Complete the sentences by adding a subordinate clause.

a. It started to rain, so _____.

b. When _____, they hid behind a large rock.

c. We go to our music lesson then _____.

d. Because _____, the driver went very fast.

SENTENCES

Complex Sentences 2

A **complex sentence** is made up of a principal clause and a subordinate clause. They can be joined by a relative pronoun. (Examples: She is a person *who* <u>is very fond of animals</u>. This is the costume *that* <u>I will wear on stage</u>.)

I'll use *which* and *that* to talk about animals and things.

I'll use *who* to talk about people.

1. Complete the subordinate clauses.

a. A doctor is a person who _____.

b. I have a book, which _____.

c. These are the boys who _____.

d. I want you to know that _____.

e. You'll never guess who _____!

f. This is my new bike, which _____.

2. Use *which, that,* or *who* to fill the gaps. (Hint: The word *which* is used for "extra information." It follows a comma.)

a. A pilot is a person _____ flies planes.

b. Here is your hat, _____ you left in the playground.

c. This is the picture _____ I have been painting.

d. It was a song _____ everybody was singing.

e. This is my book, _____ you may like to read.

f. The townspeople cheered the men _____ had put out the fire.

SENTENCES

Adverbial Clauses 1

Many subordinate clauses do the work of adverbs. They are called **adverbial clauses**. (Examples: He went to bed <u>because he was very tired</u>. I will buy a football <u>when I have enough money</u>.)

Adverbial clauses tell us more about the verb. They tell us:
how   where   when   why

Conjunctions link them to the principal clause.

1. Note what the adverbial clause tells us—*how, when, where,* or *why*.

a. I will make the toast, while Dad cooks the eggs.   _____

b. Noriko knows a great spot where we can have a picnic.   _____

c. After I get dressed for school, I will make my lunch.   _____

d. You can't go in because you haven't got a ticket.   _____

e. I will come as fast as I can.   _____

f. My dog follows me wherever I go.   _____

g. Although she played well, she was not picked for the team.   _____

h. I am not going unless you come with me.   _____

i. We cheered until all the players left the field.   _____

j. When the tide goes out, we will pick up shells on the sand.   _____

2. Write the conjunctions from the above sentences. Then search them out here.

_____

_____

_____

_____

_____

_____

_____

_____

S	F	P	T	N	C	J	O	K	R
D	W	H	E	R	E	V	E	R	B
Y	H	G	Y	P	F	Q	I	H	D
U	E	B	E	C	A	U	S	E	E
U	N	L	E	S	S	I	R	U	R
E	T	I	E	L	T	E	E	O	E
L	I	T	H	Q	R	T	T	R	H
I	F	N	E	P	O	W	F	J	W
H	G	U	O	H	T	L	A	P	Y
W	L	O	W	X	S	H	P	E	D

SENTENCES

Adverbial Clauses 2

Adverbial clauses tell us more about the verb in a sentence. Conjunctions link them to the principal clause. (Examples: Joe stood up, <u>so</u> the old lady could sit down. I will come to the party <u>when</u> I have finished weight training.)

1. Underline the adverbial clauses. Circle the conjunctions.

a. The man did not speak until everyone was quiet.

b. When I broke my leg, I had to use crutches.

c. Don't play in the sun unless you wear a hat.

d. You must think before you speak.

e. Our class went to the library then to the pool.

f. Mom said that I couldn't go because I was too young.

g. Whenever you can come, I will be happy to see you.

h. I'll stay here while you get your backpack.

2. Write the correct conjunctions below.

a. I'll eat the soup _____ it is hot.

b. _____ you go to the shop, will you get me a dozen eggs?

c. We couldn't see _____ the lights went out.

d. Simon knows a place _____ we can pitch our tent.

e. _____ he hurt his knee, he continued to play the game.

although	after	where	before
while	unless	because	when

SENTENCES

Adjectival Clauses

Many subordinate clauses do the work of adjectives. They are called **adjectival clauses**. (Examples: She is a person <u>who likes animals</u>. I am buying the game <u>that was advertised on TV</u>.)

I'll use *which* and *that* to talk about animals and things.

I'll use *who* to talk about people.

Adjectival clauses always follow the noun they describe.

1. Underline the noun or pronoun that the adjectival clause describes.

a. The horse, which he bought for $1,000, became a great racehorse.

b. Everyone who could sing joined the choir.

c. He gave her a necklace that was made from gold and diamonds.

d. The people, who had been waiting for a long time, were pleased to see the train.

e. An hour before the shop closed, all the meat that was left was reduced in price.

2. Add *who*, *which*, or *that* to complete the clauses.

a. The movie showed the men _____ first landed on the moon.

b. The cattle dog, _____ is now very old, rounded up all the stray cows.

c. This is the tree house _____ took us two weeks to build.

d. I didn't know the person _____ knocked on the door.

e. We visited the zoo to see the polar bear _____ had just been born.

3. Use *who*, *which*, and *that* in sentences of your own.

a. _____

b. _____

c. _____

SENTENCES

Sentences in Dialogue 1

Sentences can record the speech of one person to another. This is called **dialogue**. Look at the examples below.

"I went to Alaska last week," said Jill.

"Was it cold there?" asked Byron.

Speech is written in <u>present</u>, <u>past</u>, or <u>future</u> tense.

<u>Quotation marks</u> are placed around the spoken words.

1. Underline the spoken words in this dialogue.

"Dad's taking us across the town by train this holiday," said Jessica excitedly. "Where are you going, Eddie?"

"We're going to stay in a hotel, just south of Sydney," Eddie replied. "We'll be right beside the beach."

"That sounds fun, too," said Jessica. "We should get some great photos."

"Yeah, Mom has just bought a digital camera, and she wants to try it out," said Eddie. Then he smiled, "She's not very good with techno things, though."

2. Write the spoken words in the boxes below. Go back and put quotation marks around the spoken words.

a. _____ begged Carlie.

b. _____ cried Baby Bear.

c. _____ the waiter said politely.

d. _____ the captain warned his team.

e. _____ I said, wiping my hands on my apron.

Who didn't do their homework?	Let me show you the menu,
Please come to the movies with me,	Who has been sleeping in my bed?
We'll need to score an early goal,	Just stir in the flour slowly,

SENTENCES

Sentences in Dialogue 2

Spoken words are separated from unspoken words by a comma, question mark, or exclamation mark. Look at the examples below.

"Let's take the dog for a walk," said Tom.

"Where do you want to go?" asked James.

1. Punctuate these questions and answers.

- Underline the spoken words.
- Put quotation marks around the spoken words.
- Separate the spoken words from the unspoken words.

a. What game do you want to play asked Jeremy

Why don't we have a game of marbles answered Karl

b. Michael called out Has anyone seen my football

No Michael shouted everyone altogether

c. Where is the nearest shop asked the man from Africa

Do you want me to take you asked Jack

2. Now write a question and answer of your own.

_____

_____

3. Punctuate this dialogue. (Reminder: Each new speaker has a new line.)

How was your first day back at school Aunt Jean asked

It was great said Sally My teacher's name is Ms. Fiz and I sat beside my best friend

What was the best thing you did today Aunt Jean asked

Sally said the teacher took photos of all the children She told us that we would be writing a little bit about ourselves to go in a class book

That sounds interesting said Aunt Jean

SENTENCES

Assessment - Sentences

CHECK 1: **Check only the sentences.** ☐ /5

    a. up the road and over the hill ☐

    b. Collecting rocks is my hobby. ☐

    c. a bucket of golf balls ☐

    d. a blue skateboard and a red scooter ☐

    e. Far away, lies the island of Hawaii. ☐

CHECK 2: **Write "Fact" or "Opinion" beside the following statements.** ☐ /5

    a. The United States has fifty states. _____

    b. Red cars are faster than black ones. _____

    c. There are 26 letters in the English alphabet. _____

    d. All dogs can be trained to fetch a newspaper. _____

    e. Male birds are more colorful than female birds. _____

CHECK 3: **Write and punctuate five questions.** ☐ /5

    a. Where _____

    b. Who _____

    c. How _____

    d. When _____

    e. Why _____

SENTENCES

CHECK 4:   Circle the verbs in these commands.   ☐ /5

   a. Play a tune on your violin, please.

   b. Cut a piece of string about 30 inches long.

   c. Wash your fruit before eating it.

   d. Slice some cheese for our sandwiches, please.

   e. Toss the ball high above your head.

CHECK 5:   Draw a box around the subject in each sentence.   ☐ /5

   a. The circus clown is wearing baggy green trousers.

   b. After the storm, muddy, brown water filled the dam.

   c. From far away came the sound of rumbling thunder.

   d. With a screech of brakes, the car stopped at the red light.

   e. A tawny, gray owl perched high in the tree.

CHECK 6:   Join these compound sentences. Use *and*, *but*, or *so*.   ☐ /5

   a. I am going now, _____ Casey is coming with me.

   b. They waited for 20 minutes, _____ the bus did not come.

   c. I am feeling hot, _____ I will switch on the fan.

   d. Kym bought a pair of shoes, _____ she also bought a pair of socks.

   e. I would read you a funny story, _____ I left my book at home.

CHECK 7:   Circle the principal clause and underline the subordinate clause.

   a. The twins were very excited when they opened their presents.   ☐ /5

   b. This is the grandfather clock that was in my uncle's house.

   c. Because his ankle was sore, he could not join in the game.

   d. There is the man who was elected senator.

   e. Until it rained, there was no water in the tank.

SENTENCES

CHECK 8: **Add an adverbial clause. You will need a conjunction, too.** ☐ /3

    a. He is sunburned _____.

    b. The race will start _____.

    c. My dog follows me _____.

CHECK 9: **Add *who*, *which*, or *that* to complete the adjectival clauses.** ☐ /3

    a. Emily is the only one _____ has completed her work.

    b. This is the poem _____ I wrote for you.

    c. The snake, _____ had been lying under the log, slithered past me.

CHECK 10: Punctuate this short dialogue. ☐ /2

Why are you boys so late coming back to class the teacher asked

Ben replied We were in the library and didn't hear the bell

CHECK 11: Punctuate the following text. ☐ /7

    Mozart was a talented musician He was born in
Austria two hundred and fifty years ago He was a
clever little boy Mozart soon learned to play the piano
He wrote many wonderful pieces of music

    Many people believe Mozart to be the greatest
composer who has ever lived I would agree with
them

Student Name: _____

Date: _____

Total Score: _____/50

SENTENCES

TARGETING GRAMMAR

GAMES & ACTIVITIES

©Teacher Created Resources, Inc.

Wordworks

This set of materials is designed for use by students, working
independently or in pairs, to improve their knowledge
(and language) of grammar.

Teachers (and helpers) train, monitor,
scaffold, and intervene as needed.
During each session, students are
encouraged to use their dictionaries.

A *Wordworks* record of achievement
matrix can be maintained as a
personal record of cards completed by
students.

The emphasis is always on learning
and reflecting on that learning, not on
the number of cards completed by any
one student.

Students will become familiar with the terms:

- Verbal adjectives
- Antonyms
- Compound words
- Definitions
- Adjectives
- Nouns
- Pronouns
- Adverbs
- Gender
- Plurals
- Collective nouns
- Contractions
- Homographs
- Possessive nouns
- Subjects
- Adjectival phrases
- Adverbial phrases
- Verbs (doing)
- Verbs (saying)
- Tense

Preparing the Materials

1. Copy the task cards (pages 125–129) onto cardstock and laminate for durability.
2. Cut out the cards and store in a small box. (A gift box is ideal.)
3. Copy, cut, and store the information on this page with the materials.
4. Copy the progress chart (page 124), sufficient for one per student. Have students glue the charts into workbooks where they will record their answers.
5. As a card is completed and corrected, the student colors the corresponding number on the progress chart.

PROGRESS CHART — *Wordworks*   Name:

1	2	3	4	5	6	7	8	9	10	11	12	13	14	15

16	17	18	19	20	21	22	23	24	25	26	27	28	29	30

PROGRESS CHART — *Wordworks*   Name:

1	2	3	4	5	6	7	8	9	10	11	12	13	14	15

16	17	18	19	20	21	22	23	24	25	26	27	28	29	30

PROGRESS CHART — *Wordworks*   Name:

1	2	3	4	5	6	7	8	9	10	11	12	13	14	15

16	17	18	19	20	21	22	23	24	25	26	27	28	29	30

PROGRESS CHART — *Wordworks*   Name:

1	2	3	4	5	6	7	8	9	10	11	12	13	14	15

16	17	18	19	20	21	22	23	24	25	26	27	28	29	30

1 VERBAL ADJECTIVES
Find matching nouns.

- buttered
- protected
- washing
- scented
- fading
- caring
- dancing
- unfinished
- training
- garbled

- work
- colors
- person
- run
- bread
- flowers
- animal
- message
- shoes
- machine

Wordworks

2 ANTONYMS
Match words of opposite meaning.

- lost
- fresh
- smooth
- late
- tall
- old
- blunt
- green
- high
- east

- rough
- sharp
- west
- ripe
- found
- early
- low
- young
- stale
- short

Wordworks

3 DEFINING NOUNS
Match the noun with its definition.

- tennis
- caravan
- laces
- bonnet
- tripod
- pumpkin
- panther
- parcel
- cello
- court

- vegetable grown on a vine
- hat tied under the chin
- game played with racquets
- stringed instrument
- black, wild animal
- strings to tie up shoes
- place to play tennis
- a group of vehicles
- three-legged camera stand
- a package

Wordworks

4 COMPOUND WORDS
Join two words to make a new one.

- fire
- home
- horse
- water
- drive
- bed
- basket
- pop
- snow
- corn

- way
- fall
- storm
- ball
- back
- wood
- work
- flakes
- side
- corn

Wordworks

5 ADJECTIVES AND NOUNS
Find matching words.

- slithering
- crunchy
- humorous
- sharp
- autumn
- dangerous
- heavy
- elderly
- sour
- joyful

- celebration
- story
- lemons
- person
- leaves
- snake
- sword
- apple
- animal
- rainfall

Wordworks

6 NOUNS AND ADJECTIVES
Sort the nouns and adjectives.

- lazy
- napkin
- court
- knuckle
- dependent
- active
- flavor
- sensible
- magical
- doorbell

- curious
- bundle
- handsome
- mystery
- enchanted
- chore
- famous
- robust
- tower
- youth

Wordworks

7 NOUNS AND VERBS
Sort the nouns and verbs.

- settle
- meddle
- riddle
- trouble
- fumble
- rattle
- jungle
- mangle
- kettle
- pimple

8 POSSESSIVE NOUNS
the house of Jack = Jack's house

- the car of Dad = _____
- the books of the teachers = _____
- the window of the bus = _____
- the bridles of the horses = _____
- the coats of the children = _____
- the collars of the dogs = _____
- the act of the clown = _____
- the end of the day = _____

9 NOUNS TO ADJECTIVES
Change the nouns
to adjectives, using "y."
Note the doubling rule
and the "final e" rule.

- frost
- run
- taste
- spot
- lump
- slime
- hand
- snap
- rose
- grit
- fish
- mist

10 ADJECTIVES TO ADVERBS
Change the adjectives
to adverbs, using "–ly."
Note the rules for "y" and "final e."

- noisy
- happy
- glad
- merry
- swift
- wide
- quick
- feeble
- lazy
- prompt
- flat
- light

11 PAST TENSE VERBS
Write the past tense form
of each verb.

- do
- jump
- has
- find
- race
- cry
- hop
- stay
- is
- fall
- sit
- change

12 ADDING –ING
Note the doubling rule
and the "final e" rule.

- hop
- face
- dry
- flow
- sit
- depend
- stumble
- crush
- roar
- admit
- confide
- ski

13 NOUNS AND VERBS

Sort into the correct columns.

- angel
- prance
- sharpen
- tale
- grind
- juggle
- pie
- fail
- statue
- flesh
- jungle
- melt
- pickle
- graze
- gallop
- violin
- swelter
- prince
- basin
- spill

14 NOUNS

Suggest a suitable noun.

- a sweet, juicy _____
- a long, narrow_____
- a kind, friendly_____
- a hard, wooden_____
- a short, funny _____
- an old, unpainted _____
- one last, desperate _____
- an ugly, bearded_____
- fresh, tasty _____
- a red, plastic _____
- a long and tedious_____

Wordworks

15 "DOING" VERBS

Write three action verbs for each noun phrase.

- wild horses _____ _____ _____
- autumn leaves _____ _____ _____
- football players _____ _____ _____
- ballet dancers _____ _____ _____
- school children _____ _____ _____
- mighty eagles _____ _____ _____
- old friends _____ _____ _____
- trained athletes _____ _____ _____
- country streams _____ _____ _____
- roving sharks _____ _____ _____

Wordworks

16 PRONOUNS

Add a pronoun.

James opened the box. _____ spread Claire's new dress on the bed. _____ was very beautiful. _____ was made of gold and silver satin. There was even a gold ribbon for _____ hair. When Claire saw it, _____ eyes shone. "_____ is the most beautiful dress _____ have ever seen. _____ shall treasure _____ always," _____ said.

she	*it*	*he*	*her*	*I*

Wordworks

17 ADJECTIVAL PHRASES

Complete the sentences with a phrase.
(e.g., The cup on the sink is clean.)

- The horse *in* _____ stumbled and fell.
- The bell *above* _____ is made of brass.
- Help me carry this box *of* _____.
- Alex chose the cake *with* _____.
- The man *by* _____ is blind.
- The tigers *at* _____ are very fierce.
- The magazine *on* _____ is interesting.
- He bought a dog *with* _____.

Wordworks

18 PLURALS

Write the plural form of the following.

- road _____
- peach _____
- lady _____
- bone _____
- body _____
- tooth _____
- potato _____
- leaf _____
- monkey _____
- goose _____

Wordworks

19 ADVERBIAL PHRASES

Complete the sentences with a phrase telling *how*, *where*, or *when* about the verb.

- Put your books on _____.
- They went to the beach last _____.
- With _____, the old man stood up.
- After _____, we went home for lunch.
- We all wore crazy hats to _____.
- The newspaper is printed every _____.
- Cars should be driven with _____.
- The police officer walked towards _____.
- During _____, we swim every day.

Wordworks

20 SUBJECT SEARCH

Circle the subject of each sentence (noun or pronoun).

- The football coach selected his team.
- Frightened, the young deer ran away.
- He couldn't find his lost kitten.
- In two days, the boys built a hideout.
- I hear a possum on the roof at night.
- On Fridays, Kate and Sue go to ballet.
- Old rusty cans lie in the garbage dump.
- The gymnasts practice on Mondays.
- "Where have you been?" asked Max.
- A tree snake slithered over the rock.

Wordworks

21 WORDS SORTS

Sort the words into four categories:

Male   Female   Either   Neither

- cow
- gander
- cabbage
- partner
- stallion
- cousin
- cyclone
- niece
- mountain
- adult
- rooster
- husband
- doe
- shack
- mare
- computer
- gymnast
- nephew
- pilot
- aunt

Wordworks

22 CONTRACTIONS

What words do these take the place of?

- can't
- hasn't
- I've
- we'll
- they'd
- we're
- you've
- she'd
- he's
- they've
- you'll
- we'd
- it's
- won't
- she's
- he'll

Wordworks

23 VERBS

Sort the verbs into "saying" or "doing."

- murmured
- sprinted
- giggled
- stammered
- stumbled
- mentioned
- clambered
- sighed
- tittered
- wandered
- lazed
- scoffed
- sailed
- commented
- feasted
- sheltered

Wordworks

24 HOMOGRAPHS

(same word, different meaning)
Write <u>two</u> meanings for each word.

- bear
- rock
- match
- orange
- light
- fire

Wordworks

25 NOUN SORTS

Animal   Person   Place   Thing

- beach
- chimpanzee
- athlete
- shovel
- comedian
- panda
- fence
- theater
- otter
- scissors
- pilot
- Italy
- zebra
- ladder
- usher
- lantern
- ranger
- kitchen
- donkey
- stadium

Wordworks

26 ANTONYMS

Match words of opposite meaning.

- tame
- ugly
- honest
- tidy
- fast
- busy
- straight
- long
- wide
- proud
- crooked
- short
- idle
- ashamed
- wild
- narrow
- slow
- untidy
- beautiful
- dishonest

Wordworks

27 COLLECTIVE NOUNS

- a herd of _____
- a pod of _____
- a clutch of _____
- a flock of _____
- a litter of _____
- a pride of _____
- a swarm of _____
- a pack of _____
- a mob of _____
- an army of _____

Wordworks

28 HELPING VERBS

Add a helper to the verb.

- I _____ see without glasses.
- He _____ not know what to say.
- She _____ playing hockey yesterday.
- They _____ spent all their money.
- We _____ eat dinner at 7:00 tonight.
- Mrs. Jones _____ just driven past.
- Marty _____ waiting outside for you.
- _____ you read this book yet?
- _____ you give me your ruler, please?
- _____ they gone to the game?

Wordworks

29 ADJECTIVE SORTS

Sort into three categories:
Person   Place   Thing

- rocky
- calm
- shady
- broken
- athletic
- deserted
- chewy
- young
- sparkling
- kind
- sandy
- crumpled
- crowded
- clever
- plastic
- curious
- shiny
- restful

Wordworks

30 CONTRACTIONS

Contract these subjects and verbs.

- She will
- I have
- He is
- They would
- You are
- We have
- I would
- They are
- She would
- I am
- It is
- He will
- You have
- We are

Wordworks

Shuffle 'n' Sort

Shuffle 'n' Sort is a set of materials designed for use by a whole class, with students working in pairs. It supports the development of grammatical knowledge and vocabulary. Dictionary skills support this work.

Preparation of Materials

① Copy the baseboard (page 132) onto cardstock and laminate for durability. You will need one per pair of students.

② Copy each page of words (pages 133–152) onto cardstock. Laminate for durability.

③ Cut out all the words on a page and store in an envelope. Clearly mark the envelope with a number (1–20).

Tip 1: It is helpful to also label the number of the envelope onto the back of each word card, so that cards can be returned to their correct envelope.

Tip 2: Place a piece of sticky tape over the adhesive on the envelope, so students can't seal the envelope after use.

④ Copy the Progress Chart (page 131), sufficient for one per student. Ask students to glue their charts into specified workbooks.

Using the Materials

① Each pair selects a Shuffle 'n' Sort envelope and a baseboard.

② The students first place the three large words on the baseboard, one above each column.

③ Students then categorize the remaining words under these three categories. Suggest that they sort those they know first, and then refer to a dictionary for the meaning of those they don't know.

Tip: If only one student in the pair knows a meaning, it is their job to "teach" their partner.

④ It is the teacher's job at this point to circulate among the students, answering questions, offering advice, and capitalizing on those "teachable moments."

Tip: It is helpful to engage the support of teacher aides or volunteer adults.

⑤ Teachers need to check cards on completion for accuracy and understanding.

⑥ Both students then color the numbers (located on their envelope) on their progress charts.

Optional Extra

When words have been sorted into their categories, ask the students to write up to three sentences, perhaps using a word from each category.

PROGRESS CHART   **Shuffle 'n' Sort**   Name:

1	2	3	4	5	6	7	8	9	10	11	12	13	14	15

16	17	18	19	20	21	22	23	24	25	26	27	28	29	30

PROGRESS CHART   **Shuffle 'n' Sort**   Name:

1	2	3	4	5	6	7	8	9	10	11	12	13	14	15

16	17	18	19	20	21	22	23	24	25	26	27	28	29	30

PROGRESS CHART   **Shuffle 'n' Sort**   Name:

1	2	3	4	5	6	7	8	9	10	11	12	13	14	15

16	17	18	19	20	21	22	23	24	25	26	27	28	29	30

PROGRESS CHART   **Shuffle 'n' Sort**   Name:

1	2	3	4	5	6	7	8	9	10	11	12	13	14	15

16	17	18	19	20	21	22	23	24	25	26	27	28	29	30

	BASEBOARD	

Shuffle 'n' Sort

 ©Teacher Created Resources, Inc.

HEAR	TOUCH	SEE
chortle	caress	survey
whistle	clutch	glance
jangle	brush	search
whimper	grasp	stare
chatter	hold	peek
whisper	pinch	regard
cheer	press	glimpse
squeal	rub	recognize
scream	scrape	observe
clatter	scratch	squint
giggle	squeeze	view
clang	stroke	notice

Shuffle 'n' Sort Number 1

SOUND	SMELL	TOUCH
deafening	putrid	slimy
audible	fragrant	greasy
quiet	perfumed	rough
noisy	sweet	lumpy
piercing	scented	smooth
shrill	rank	coarse
deep	pungent	silky
high-pitched	musty	tepid
faint	aromatic	flabby
echoing	acrid	firm
melodious	fresh	moist
bass	moldy	slippery

Shuffle 'n' Sort Number 2

PERSON	PLACE	THING
doctor	garden	cymbal
comedian	theater	fingernail
astronaut	Saturn	carafe
acrobat	supermarket	axle
jockey	dungeon	saddle
waiter	café	certificate
musician	arena	cage
tourist	ranch	staircase
ranger	stadium	wardrobe
traveler	auditorium	microphone
contestant	laboratory	computer
priest	cathedral	goblet

Shuffle 'n' Sort Number 3

NOUN	VERB	ADJECTIVE
armchair	take	favorite
highway	stretch	sticky
person	disturb	thoughtful
turbulence	imagine	careless
seascape	disappoint	strong
factory	speak	delicate
handstand	loiter	stunning
refinery	unlock	fantastic
trowel	decide	gloomy
business	win	charming
petroleum	repeat	responsible
document	discover	wholesome

Shuffle 'n' Sort Number 4

PEOPLE ("Describing" Adjectives)	PLACE ("Describing" Adjectives)	THING ("Describing" Adjectives)
sensible	sandy	flimsy
confident	rocky	shimmering
serious	leafy	plastic
frightened	shady	painted
interested	secluded	juicy
nosy	deserted	ripe
likeable	crowded	yellow
friendly	stony	buttered
handsome	cozy	tasty
mischievous	roomy	golden
sporty	safe	shiny
kind	snowy	empty

Shuffle 'n' Sort Number 5

PEOPLE	PLACES	THINGS
aviator	arena	test
escapee	mansion	radio
president	grotto	cushion
detective	China	accordion
guide	palace	pencil
soldier	pasture	barometer
artist	gallery	quilt
cowboy	swamp	helicopter
guard	studio	lantern
clown	church	skirt
princess	stable	dust
journalist	castle	trophy

Shuffle 'n' Sort Number 6

©Teacher Created Resources, Inc.

Could SPILL	Could BREAK	Could TEAR
jelly beans	egg	paper
medicine	bottle	fabric
flour	cup	jeans
milk	window	curtain
vinegar	promise	cardboard
coffee	statue	stamp
salt	vase	book
oil	heart	cushion
sugar	ruler	skirt
lemonade	toy	ticket
cinnamon	arm	bedsheet
pepper	bread	lettuce

Shuffle 'n' Sort Number 7

PRESENT	PAST	FUTURE
somersault	attended	will fly
is skidding	separated	will spend
wakes	brought	will eat
packs	went	shall dance
is falling	was playing	may go
come	knocked	will cook
chimes	has been	might live
is selling	sprinted	shall see
bring	caught	may run
borrows	were doing	will stand
does	ran	might fight
are stopping	had done	will study

Shuffle 'n' Sort Number 8

COLOR	SHAPE	SIZE
scarlet	oval	large
crimson	triangular	enormous
aqua	square	tiny
russet	oblong	gigantic
orange	tapered	little
azure	lopsided	thick
pink	rounded	narrow
brownish	potbellied	wide
earthy	circular	huge
aquamarine	bent	undersized
pastel	crooked	small
yellowed	straight	average

Shuffle 'n' Sort Number 9

©Teacher Created Resources, Inc.   141   #2435 Targeting Grammar

DOING	BEING/HAVING	SAYING
cycle	have	mumble
sprint	is	murmur
paddle	are	mutter
write	had	sputter
guide	has been	sigh
guard	was	gabble
throw	were	inform
travel	was being	notify
rinse	am	declare
push	are having	whisper
study	have had	whimper
unpack	was having	gossip

Shuffle 'n' Sort Number 10

WHO	WHEN	WHERE
athlete	century	signpost
gardener	moment	clue
uncle	recess	pointer
dentist	quarter	bookmark
sailor	semester	beacon
consultant	season	label
hairdresser	generation	tag
lawyer	lifetime	arrow
florist	millennium	location
archer	part-time	site
pitcher	contract	indicator
officer	full-time	directions

Shuffle 'n' Sort Number 11

SAY	THINK	FEEL
grumble	muse	love
swear	remember	adore
mumble	consider	praise
grunt	ponder	trust
verbalize	decide	ignore
stutter	puzzle	attract
protest	wonder	celebrate
rant	presume	worry
rave	contemplate	hope
declare	reminisce	respect
state	solve	admire
persuade	memorize	sympathize

Shuffle 'n' Sort Number 12

HE	SHE	THEY
husband	ballerina	jury
nephew	lass	tribe
lad	dame	club
knight	countess	swarm
gnome	bride	class
prince	ewe	flock
groom	soprano	clan
rooster	vixen	audience
mister	mare	group
duke	queen	herd
baritone	maiden	fleet
gander	squaw	band

Shuffle 'n' Sort Number 13

ROUND	TALL	LONG
orange	steeple	avenue
volleyball	skyscraper	boulevard
globe	giraffe	street
balloon	mountain	string
clock	tree	twine
button	tower	rope
pizza	windmill	river
hoop	escalator	esplanade
beads	chimney	alley
peas	smokestack	anaconda
wheel	pyramid	footpath
drum	ladder	boa

Shuffle 'n' Sort Number 14

HAPPY	SAD	ANGRY
jolly	dejected	fiery
pleased	forlorn	sullen
contented	somber	furious
joyous	downcast	fierce
cheerful	sorrowful	sulky
excited	distressed	frantic
jovial	wistful	resentful
satisfied	dismal	savage
overjoyed	gloomy	agitated
delighted	miserable	wild
merry	glum	irate
glad	desolate	violent

Shuffle 'n' Sort Number 15

BIRD	ANIMAL	REPTILE
pelican	wombat	gecko
wren	platypus	viper
falcon	possum	python
pigeon	buffalo	skink
penguin	cheetah	alligator
vulture	rattlesnake	lizard
flamingo	badger	cobra
ostrich	gorilla	tortoise
emu	stallion	crocodile
parrot	groundhog	snake
magpie	leopard	iguana
ibis	bear	chameleon

Shuffle 'n' Sort Number 16

PEOPLE ("Describing" Adjectives)	PEOPLE ("Saying" Verbs)	PEOPLE ("Moving" Verbs)
healthy	snicker	crawl
beautiful	whisper	creep
blind	scoff	stumble
modest	complain	hobble
chubby	scold	flee
lonely	mock	hurry
tedious	warn	trudge
dishonest	drone	plod
elegant	joke	limp
polite	brag	waddle
greedy	threaten	pursue
confident	boast	sprint

Shuffle 'n' Sort Number 17

SEA	LAND	AIR
whale	plateau	clouds
coral	avalanche	thunder
shells	valley	lightning
reef	gorge	mist
shark	volcano	fog
oyster	canyon	meteor
prawns	glacier	comet
dolphin	boulder	satellite
waves	river	helicopter
seaweed	canyon	moon
stingray	peninsula	planet
jellyfish	butte	storm

Shuffle 'n' Sort Number 18

BIRD	ANIMAL	INSECT
flamingo	jaguar	cicada
parrot	llama	locust
heron	leopard	dragonfly
stork	hyena	hornet
swan	beaver	louse
puffin	stallion	midge
toucan	otter	flea
seagull	colt	mosquito
penguin	cougar	tick
turkey	mare	beetle
pigeon	antelope	wasp
peacock	camel	ant

Shuffle 'n' Sort Number 19

NOUN	VERB	ADJECTIVE
feather	elect	familiar
kiosk	baffle	hazy
dwarf	capture	punctual
almond	publish	odd
biography	occupy	numb
anthem	mope	moody
orphan	lunge	lukewarm
nursery	vibrate	majestic
shield	applaud	jaunty
beret	whine	empty
scarf	narrate	sly
jellyfish	shuffle	stormy

Shuffle 'n' Sort Number 20

Fact Finders

Fact Finders is a set of materials designed for use by a whole class, with students working in pairs. It supports the development of language use, vocabulary, and grammar. Dictionary skills support this work.

Preparation of Materials

1. Copy all the materials (pages 155–184) onto cardstock. Laminate for durability.

2. Cut out the Fact Finders cards (pages 170–184), and stack in a box.

3. Cut out the Fact Finders words and meanings (pages 155–169). There are eight words/meanings per set, with a number corresponding to a Fact Finders card. Place these in envelopes and clearly number them. Store the envelopes in the box with the Fact Finders cards. (*Tip*: Place a strip of sticky tape over the adhesive on the envelope, so students can't seal the envelope after use.)

4. Copy the Progress Chart (page 154), sufficient for one per student. Ask each student to glue it into a specified workbook where they will record their answers.

Using the Materials

1. Each pair selects a Fact Finders card and corresponding envelope.

2. The students first place the words in alphabetical order.

3. Students match the meanings to the words. Suggest that they match those they know first and then refer to a dictionary for those they don't. (*Tip*: If only one student knows a meaning, it is his or her job to "teach" their partner.)

4. When words and meanings are matched, ask students to use them to complete the work on the Fact Finders card. Although they may confer, both students write their own answers. It is the teacher's job at this point to circulate among the students, answering questions, offering advice, and capitalizing on those "teachable moments." (*Tip*: It is helpful to engage the support of teacher aides or volunteer adults.)

5. Teachers need to check cards on completion for accuracy and understanding.

6. Both students then color the corresponding number (located on the envelope) on their progress charts.

7. All word and meaning cards are returned to the envelope. The envelope and card are filed back in the Fact Finders box.

PROGRESS CHART ## Fact Finders Name:

1	2	3	4	5	6	7	8	9	10	11	12	13	14	15

16	17	18	19	20	21	22	23	24	25	26	27	28	29	30

PROGRESS CHART ## Fact Finders Name:

1	2	3	4	5	6	7	8	9	10	11	12	13	14	15

16	17	18	19	20	21	22	23	24	25	26	27	28	29	30

PROGRESS CHART ## Fact Finders Name:

1	2	3	4	5	6	7	8	9	10	11	12	13	14	15

16	17	18	19	20	21	22	23	24	25	26	27	28	29	30

PROGRESS CHART ## Fact Finders Name:

1	2	3	4	5	6	7	8	9	10	11	12	13	14	15

16	17	18	19	20	21	22	23	24	25	26	27	28	29	30

Fact Finders 1

hangar	a large shed for planes
herd	a number of animals together
hibernate	sleep through winter
history	story of past events
pancake	a thin, flat cake
parachute	used to slow a fall from a plane
profession	job requiring skill and training
punctual	being on time

Fact Finders 2

congratulate	to wish joy to a person
glimmer	to shine faintly
humorous	funny
jockey	rider of a racehorse
knuckle	a finger joint
lettuce	green plant used in salads
odor	a smell
wardrobe	all the clothes belonging to someone

dinosaur	huge reptile (no longer living)
dough	unbaked bread or cookies
label	tag with a name on it
mirror	a looking glass
orchard	garden for growing fruit
raft	floating platform of logs
shrub	a bush
somersault	turn heels over head

Fact Finders 4

banjo	musical instrument with strings
chestnut	a reddish-brown color
cinnamon	a spice used as flavoring
lounge	to behave lazily
massive	large and heavy
swan	waterbird with long neck
syrup	thick, brown, sugary liquid
venom	the poison of snakes

Fact Finders 5

absent	away, not present
baboon	a large monkey
gravel	small stones and coarse sand
massage	soothe muscles/joints by rubbing
publish	print and sell copies of a book
sunflower	tall, flowering plant with seeds
village	group of houses
wan	looking pale and weak

Fact Finders 6

clamber	climb with hands and feet
plaque	coating on teeth causing decay
pyramid	object with triangular sides
recipe	instructions for cooking food
sawdust	wood dust made by sawing
starboard	right side of a ship
tender	delicate, soft, or gentle
warp	twist out of shape

collie	a dog bred to herd sheep
dentist	person trained to treat teeth
khaki	dull greenish-brown color
racquet	bat used in playing tennis
rancid	having a sour smell or taste
tier	a row or layer
trail	a path through rough country
wilt	to become limp

Fact Finders 8

bangs	hair that falls across the forehead
blacktop	a material used for roads
buzzard	large bird like a hawk
feral	wild or untamed
jack	tool used for lifting a car
pair	two things that go together
parsnip	white root vegetable
topsy-turvy	upside down or back to front

Fact Finders 9

chess	game played on a checkered board
chord	several notes played in harmony
curb	concrete at the edge of a street
grate	to scrape or grind
original	first, new, not copied
strike	to hit, punch
whelp	a young dog, wolf, bear, or lion
whistle	shrill sound made by blowing

Fact Finders 10

comedy	amusing performance or event
dew	drops of water found on grass
draft	rough sketch, piece of writing
fort	place armed against enemy attack
leader	someone who guides others
menu	list of dishes served at a restaurant
oyster	shellfish you can eat
steal	take something that is not yours

Fact Finders 11

cherry	small, juicy fruit with a pit
crow	a big, black bird
rattle	make short, sharp, clattering sound
stampede	sudden rush by people or animals
tidbit	small, delicious piece of food
venue	place where an event is held
witch	woman who practices magic
wrap	fold paper or material around

Fact Finders 12

antenna	television aerial
brooch	ornament pinned on clothes
forage	to search around for food
password	secret word to gain entry
population	people living in a country
portrait	picture/painting of one's face
severe	extremely bad or dangerous
taut	stretched very tight

Fact finders 13

cyclone	storm that moves in a circle
cymbals	round, brass clappers used in a band
ignore	take no notice of
mimic	to copy someone or something
octagonal	having eight sides
robot	machine that moves like a human
secret	something hidden, private
thorn	sharp prickle/spike on a plant

Fact Finders 14

bulldozer	tractor with blade in front
carnival	a public festive occasion
fountain	place where water spurts upwards
ponder	think about deeply
poor	having very little money
stench	a very bad smell
urn	a kind of vase
wizard	someone who practices magic

brochure	information booklet
course	ground where a race takes place
gully	channel made by running water
harp	large stringed instrument
laundry	place where clothes are washed
maid	a woman servant
salad	mix of uncooked vegetables
snowflake	a flake or crystal of snow

Fact Finders 16

arena	place for sporting events
blurb	information about a book
chore	boring or unpleasant job
court	ground where tennis is played
flaw	a crack, scratch, defect
landslide	rocks/soil falling down steep slope
lava	hot liquid rock from a volcano
meter	instrument that measures (e.g., gas)

athlete	someone competing in sports
awe	great respect with a little fear
crowd	a large number of people
employee	someone who is paid to work
gosling	young goose
gradual	little by little
lazy	unwilling to work
stable	place for housing horses

Fact Finders 18

band	group of musicians
bashful	shy, timid, reserved
comrade	close friend or companion
navigate	guide the course of a vehicle
platypus	Australian native animal
promptly	done straightaway
stare	look at for a long time
vandal	person who damages property

bough	branch of a tree
broad	wide
lagoon	lake of sea water
lavender	perfumed plant; purple color
sofa	long seat with a back
tow	pull with ropes or chains
vagabond	somebody who wanders
veil	thin cloth to cover the face

Fact Finders 20

cancel	to cross out or do away with
character	someone in a story or play
forecast	to say what might happen
jaywalk	cross a street carelessly
matador	bullfighter from Spain
nimble	able to move quickly and easily
peppercorn	dried berry of black pepper plant
waterfall	water falling from a height

Fact Finders 21

bacteria	tiny living things that cause disease
cathedral	the church of a bishop
elevator	cage or platform to take people up in a building
exquisite	most excellent and beautiful
helicopter	aircraft with fan-like blades
hood	covers the engine of an automobile
mast	pole to hold up ship's sails
tire	band of rubber around a wheel

Fact Finders 22

apology	an expression of regret
charcoal	partly burnt wood
footlights	lights across the front of a stage
hamper	large basket with a lid
polo	ball game played on horseback
saddle	seat used by a horse rider
supporter	person who encourages others
turkey	large farm bird raised for food

Fact Finders 23

assortment	collection of mixed items
cabbage	leafy green vegetable
castaway	one who has been shipwrecked
estimate	to guess thoughtfully
mask	covering for eyes or face
overboard	over the side of a ship
phantom	ghost
rare	not often seen

Fact Finders 24

crackers	thin, crisp, salty snacks
honey	sweet, sticky liquid made by bees
landscape	a country scene
paperback	book with a soft cover
penniless	without any money
piece	small bit or part of something
quintuplets	five babies born at one birth
quiver	a case for holding arrows

carnivore	meat-eating animal
deluge	a heavy rain or flood
famine	a great shortage of food
fare	price paid for transportation
pendulum	swinging weight on some clocks
porridge	oats cooked with milk or water
raisins	dried fruit made from grapes
squid	sea animal with tentacles

Fact Finders 26

cocoa	chocolate-flavored powder
enormous	huge, very large
flimsy	weak, frail, thin
hemisphere	half of the Earth
orphan	child with no parents
rectangle	four-sided shape
smooth	flat and even, not rough
toadstool	poisonous fungus like a mushroom

aisle	path between seats or shelves
cucumber	long, green salad vegetable
flounce	move off with an impatient jerk
hazel	yellowy-brown color; also type of nut
knowledge	facts that are known
reluctant	unwillingness to do something
site	place where something is built
spellbound	fascinate, rapt, captivated

Fact Finders 28

calico	rough cotton cloth
diploma	paper showing graduation
florist	flower seller
portly	slightly overweight
solar	having to do with the sun
sparrow	small, brown bird
sturdy	strongly built
submarine	boat that goes under the sea

crockery	cups, saucers, plates, etc.
dandelion	weed with yellow flower
decade	a period of ten years
ginger	hot, spicy root used in cooking
glazier	one who fits glass into windows
pane	single sheet of glass
scorch	burn slightly, often with an iron
spine	backbone

Fact Finders 30

avalanche	a fall of earth, rocks, and snow
azure	soft, blue color
bridal	relating to a bride or wedding
crimson	a bright, red color
hacienda	main house on a farm in Spain
haggle	to bargain about the price
patchwork	colored squares sewn together
upstanding	erect, upright, or honorable

Fact Finders

Close in on the facts. Use the context as a clue to the missing words.

- I read about Captain Cook in my _____ book.
- Snakes _____ all through the winter.
- She would like to make teaching her _____.

Research and sketch a **parachute**.

Research and write a homophone for: **hangar**, **herd**.

Write sentences containing these words: **pancake**, **punctual**.

Fact Finders

Fact Finders

Close in on the facts. Use the context as a clue to the missing words.

- There was a _____ of light at the end of the tunnel.
- I _____ you on winning the cross-country race.
- She could not get the ring over her swollen _____.

Research and sketch a **lettuce**.

Write a word that means the same as: **odor**, **humorous**.

Write sentences containing these words: **wardrobe**, **jockey**.

Fact Finders

Fact Finders

Close in on the facts. Use the context as a clue to the missing words.

- The farmer is picking apples from the trees in his _____.
- Make sure you put a _____ on your lunchbox before the bus trip.
- Jasmine is a _____ with sweet-smelling flowers.
- You can see your reflection in a _____.

Research and sketch: a **raft**, a **dinosaur**.

Write sentences containing these words: **somersault**, **dough**.

Fact Finders

Fact Finders

Close in on the facts. Use the context as a clue to the missing words.

- The chef added a teaspoon of _____ to the dough.
- The climbers came to a _____ rock fall.
- A python is not a _____ous snake.

Research and sketch a **banjo**.

Write a different meaning for: **lounge**, **chestnut**.

Write sentences containing these words: **swan**, **syrup**.

Fact Finders

Fact Finders

5

Close in on the facts. Use the context as a clue to the missing words.

- The cattle truck bumped along the _____ road.
- The football player had a _____ to relieve his aching legs.
- J.K. Rowling has had several books _____ed.
- Months of illness left him weak and _____.

Research and sketch: a **sunflower**, a **baboon**.

Write sentences containing these words: **absent**, **village**.

Fact Finders

Fact Finders

6

Close in on the facts. Use the context as a clue to the missing words.

- The boy is _____ing up the tree to pick some ripe plums.
- The deck chairs on the ocean liner were on the _____ deck.
- Plastic objects will often _____ if they are exposed to heat.

Research and sketch a **pyramid**.

Write a different meaning for: **plaque**, **tender**.

Write sentences containing these words: **recipe**, **sawdust**.

Fact Finders

Fact Finders

7

Close in on the facts. Use the context as a clue to the missing words.

- Flowers will _____ if you do not give them water.
- The soldiers were dressed in _____ uniforms.
- Milk left out of the refrigerator will soon become _____.

Research and sketch a **racquet**.

Write a different meaning for **trail** and a homophone for **tier**.

Write sentences containing these words: **dentist**, **collie**.

Fact Finders

Fact Finders

8

Close in on the facts. Use the context as a clue to the missing words.

- We bounced the ball on the _____ at school.
- _____s flew down to feast on the dead beast.
- _____ pigs have become a big problem for farmers.

Research and sketch a girl with **bangs**.

Write a different meaning for **jack** and a homophone for **pair**.

Write sentences containing these words: **parsnip**, **topsy-turvy**.

Fact Finders

Fact Finders

9

Close in on the facts. Use the context as a clue to the missing words.

- This is an _____ oil painting, painted by Picasso.
- The car pulled into the _____, and the passenger got out.
- When I _____, my dog comes running to me.

    Research and sketch: a **chess board**, a **whelp**.

    Research and write a homophone for: **grate**, **chord**.

    Write two sentences using **strike**—first as a verb, then as a noun.

Fact Finders

Fact Finders

10

Close in on the facts. Use the context as a clue to the missing words.

- The _____ of the school was the principal.
- My poem is still in _____ form.
- I like funny movies so I selected a video from the _____ section.

    Research and sketch an **oyster**.

    Write a homophone for: **fort**, **steal**.

    Write sentences containing these words: **dew**, **menu**.

Fact Finders

Fact Finders

11

Close in on the facts. Use the context as a clue to the missing words.

- Queen's Park is the _____ for the traveling circus.
- John fed _____s of meat to his dog under the table.
- The crash of thunder caused the cattle to _____.

Research and sketch a **cherry** and a **crow**.

Research and write a homophone for: **witch**, **wrap**.

Write two sentences using **rattle**—first as a verb, then as a noun.

Fact Finders

Fact Finders

12

Close in on the facts. Use the context as a clue to the missing words.

- Dad looked at me _____ly when I broke his ruler.
- I had my _____ painted by an artist in the mall.
- Rats _____ in the garbage dump at night.

Research and sketch a television **antenna**.

Write a homophone for: **taut**, **brooch**.

Write sentences containing these words: **password**, **population**.

Fact Finders

Fact Finders

Close in on the facts. Use the context as a clue to the missing words.

- Be careful of _____s when cutting roses.
- The comedian could _____ the voices of many famous people.
- People do not _____ me when I am speaking to them.
- Jack loves to play the _____ in the brass band.

Research and sketch a **robot** and an **octagonal** table.

Write sentences containing these words: **cyclone**, **secret**.

Fact Finders

Fact Finders

14

Close in on the facts. Use the context as a clue to the missing words.

- _____s were used to clear the land for a new highway.
- The boy sat _____ing what to do when he missed the bus.
- I won several prizes at our school _____.

Research and sketch a **fountain**.

Write a homophone for: **urn**, **poor**.

Write sentences containing these words: **wizard**, **stench**.

Fact Finders

Fact Finders

Close in on the facts. Use the context as a clue to the missing words.

- During the wet weather, water runs down the _____.
- We read the travel _____ before our trip to Italy.

Write three compound words beginning with **snow**.

Research and sketch a **harp**.

Research and write a homophone for: **maid, course**.

Write sentences containing these words: **salad, laundry**.

Fact Finders

Fact Finders

16

Close in on the facts. Use the context as a clue to the missing words.

- The Grand Parade was held in the main _____.
- _____ spewed from the active volcano.
- Have you read the _____ on the back of the book?

Research and sketch a tennis **court**.

Write a homophone for: **flaw, meter**.

Write sentences containing these words: **landslide, chore**.

Fact Finders

Fact Finders

17

Close in on the facts. Use the context as a clue to the missing words.

- He is an _____ of an electronics company.
- There has been a _____ increase in the price of bread this year.
- The twins enjoyed the school holidays and being _____.

Research and sketch an **athlete** and a **gosling**.

Write a different meaning for **stable**. Write a homophone for **awe**.

Write two sentences using **crowd**—first a noun, then as a verb.

Fact Finders

Fact Finders

18

Close in on the facts. Use the context as a clue to the missing words.

- The captain had to _____ through a channel to reach the sea.
- _____s were responsible for the damage to the window.
- The work was done _____ by all the students in the class.

Sketch your best **comrade**. Write an antonym of **bashful**.

Write a different meaning for **band**.

Write sentences containing these words: **platypus**, **stare**.

Fact Finders

Fact Finders

19

Close in on the facts. Use the context as a clue to the missing words.

- The cowboy wore a hat with a _____ brim.
- The bride wore a _____ of fine white lace.
- During the summer, we went swimming in the _____.

Research and sketch a **sofa**.

Research and write a homophone for: **tow**, **bough**.

Write sentences containing these words: **lavender**, **vagabond**.

Fact Finders

Fact Finders

20

Close in on the facts. Use the context as a clue to the missing words.

- They had to _____ the race because of heavy rain.
- You must be very _____ to be a good gymnast.
- _____s are crushed and sold as ground pepper.

Research and sketch a **character** from a book you have read.

Write up to five compound words that begin with **water**.

Write sentences containing these words: **forecast**, **matador**.

Fact Finders

Fact Finders

21

Close in on the facts. Use the context as a clue to the missing words.

- The ship's _____ splintered during the violent storm.
- The _____ of the car was buckled in the accident.
- The scientist studied the _____ under the microscope.

Research and sketch a **helicopter** and an **elevator**.

Write a homophone for **tire**.

Write sentences containing these words: **exquisite**, **cathedral**.

Fact Finders

Fact Finders

22

Close in on the facts. Use the context as a clue to the missing words.

- We put our dirty clothes inside the _____ .
- Our family always has roast _____ for Thanksgiving dinner.
- You can sketch pictures with a piece of _____.

Research and sketch a football **supporter** and a **polo** player.

Write up to five compound words beginning with **foot**.

Write sentences containing these words: **apology**, **saddle**.

Fact Finders

Fact Finders

23

Close in on the facts. *Use the context as a clue to the missing words.*

- He has collected such an odd _____ of old coins.
- Can you _____ the number of jelly beans in this bottle?
- The collector was excited when he discovered a _____ stamp.

Research and sketch a **cabbage** and a **mask**.

Write up to five compound words beginning with **over**.

Write sentences containing these words: **castaway**, **phantom**.

Fact Finders

Fact Finders

24

Close in on the facts. *Use the context as a clue to the missing words.*

- The artist sat in his studio, _____ and without work.
- We always buy a lot of _____s to read on vacation.
- Slowly, she painted a beautiful _____ of the fields.

Research and sketch **quintuplets**.

Write a different meaning for **quiver**. Write a homophone for **piece**.

Write sentences containing these words: **honey**, **crackers**.

Fact Finders

Fact Finders

25

Close in on the facts. Use the context as a clue to the missing words.

- The grandfather clock ticks as the _____ swings to and fro.
- During the _____ in India, wheat was shipped in from Europe.
- The fishermen caught many _____ in their fishing nets.

Research and sketch a **carnivore**.

Research and write a homophone for: **deluge**, **fare**.

Write sentences containing these words: **porridge**, **raisins**.

Fact Finders

Fact Finders

26

Close in on the facts. Use the context as a clue to the missing words.

- The _____ed boy now lives with his uncle and aunt.
- The Southern Cross is only visible in the Southern _____.
- A whale is an _____ sea animal.

Research and sketch a **rectangle**.

Write words opposite in meaning to: **flimsy**, **smooth**.

Write sentences containing these words: **toadstool**, **cocoa**.

Fact Finders

Fact Finders

27

Close in on the facts. Use the context as a clue to the missing words.

- She is a tall girl with black hair and _____ eyes.
- Jani studies hard and has a lot of _____ about rocks.
- She stamped her foot and _____d off angrily.

Research and sketch a **cucumber**.

Research and write a homophone for: **site**, **aisle**.

Write sentences containing these words: **spellbound**, **reluctant**.

Fact Finders

Fact Finders

28

Close in on the facts. Use the context as a clue to the missing words.

- The student received his _____ after three years of study.
- We have a _____ hot water system.
- The cottage has curtains made of _____ that are tied back with ribbons.

Research and sketch a **submarine**.

Write a word opposite in meaning to: **portly**, **sturdy**.

Write sentences containing these words: **florist**, **sparrow**.

Fact Finders

Fact Finders

Close in on the facts. Use the context as a clue to the missing words.

- Something moved in the dark, and a shiver went down my _____.
- In this _____, there have been advances in computer technology.

Research and sketch three pieces of **crockery** and a **dandelion**.

Choose the correct word from these homophones:

The (**glacier**, **glazier**) inched its way toward the sea.

As he stumbled, he felt a stabbing (**pain**, **pane**) in his leg.

Write sentences containing these words: **ginger**, **scorch**.

Fact Finders

Fact Finders

Close in on the facts. Use the context as a clue to the missing words.

- The family sits on the veranda of their _____ after work.
- It is expected that you _____ over the price at a market.

Research and sketch a **patchwork** quilt.

Write three other **blue** words and three other **red** words.

Write five compound words beginning with **up**.

Write sentences containing these words: **bridal**, **avalanche**.

Fact Finders

Grammar Task Card: Nouns

1

1. Write a sentence for each noun listed.

cow	bent	rope	shuffle	see
lost	elephant	round	cart	seaweed

2. Add the apostrophes to the possessive nouns.

a. my cats paws

b. Ashars bike

c. the foxes tails

d. the cups handle

e. the students classroom

f. some birds feathers

g. the cooks saucepans

h. a bees wings

i. a teachers meeting

j. the snakes skin

3. Complete these collective nouns.

a. a _____ of sheep

b. a _____ of kangaroos

c. a _____ of fish

d. a _____ of pups

e. a _____ of ships

f. a _____ of whales

g. a _____ of eggs

h. a _____ of robbers

i. a _____ of dogs

j. a _____ of roses

Grammar Task Card: Nouns

2

1. Sort these nouns into two columns: places and things.

clouds	prison	kettle	school	tulips
waterhole	feather	cornfield	towel	church

2. Give the proper nouns capital letters.

We have a new boy in our class. His name is shahil. He came from india with his mom and dad and his sister simran. They arrived in december, just after christmas day. His father is going to teach at stanford university. I think shahil and I will be great friends because we both love to play baseball. Maybe one day, we will play for the new york yankees.

3. Complete each sentence with a noun.

a. Jane ate a sweet, juicy _____.

b. The boys climbed the tall, steep _____.

c. A bright, colorful _____ hung above the cot.

d. A shiny, red _____ came down our street.

Grammar Task Card: Nouns 3

1. Add a noun suffix to these words.

–ment	–ness	–er

a. send_____   *f.* state_____

b. good_____   *g.* kind_____

c. move_____   *h.* export_____

d. goalkeep_____   *i.* manage_____

e. ride_____   *j.* rich_____

2. Name something that is:

a. round and soft   *d.* cold and hard

b. smooth and warm   *e.* noisy

c. long and winding

Grammar Task Card: Nouns 4

1. Add "a" or "an" or "the."

a. I saw _____ children going into school.

b. Once there was _____ fierce lion.

c. I had to wait _____ hour for the bus.

d. This is _____ house I live in.

e. She has _____ orange in her lunchbox.

f. _____ horses galloped across the field.

2. Write ten compound words from the words below.

grand	time	night	head	piece	over	under
life	light	stand	father	dress	line	weight

Grammar Task Card: Adjectives   ①

1. Place an adjective before the noun.

  a. From the mountaintop, we had a _____ view.

  b. There are four _____ cars in his garage.

  c. A horse and cart went down the _____ road.

  d. A _____ bird flew overhead.

  e. We could see _____ clouds in the sky.

2. Place an adjective after the noun.

  a. The roses in the vase are _____.

  b. My pet dog is _____.

  c. The elephant is _____ and _____ .

  d. His marbles are _____.

  e. Dad was _____ when I lost the remote control.

Grammar Task Card: Adjectives   ②

1. Choose the verbal adjective in the top line to describe a noun on the bottom line.

painted	growing	chewing	ploughed	gaping	bundled
sticks	fence	plants	field	gum	hole

2. Sort these adjectives into two columns: describing people or things.

sharp	unusual	crumpled	talented	long	wealthy	thoughtful
metal	upset	friendly	heated	lonely	expensive	careless

3. Use each adjective below in a sentence.

dangerous	calendar	salty	famous	event
carnival	belt	happy	golden	library

Grammar Task Card: Adjectives 3

1. List the adjectives in this story.

The two boys reached an old, iron gate. The rusty lock fell apart when they touched it. The heavy gate swung open. The boys walked down the rough, overgrown path. An old, crumbling, sandstone house seemed to appear out of nowhere. Trembling, the two boys shone their flashlights on the falling roof and twisted shutters. A large wooden door stood open at the top of some broken stairs. It seemed to be inviting them in. Thick fog began to swirl around the boys. They were very scared.

2. Add an adjective suffix to these words.

–able	–less	–ful

a. comfort_____   *f.* tire_____

b. rest_____   *g.* reason_____

c. like_____   *h.* force_____

d. use_____   *i.* effort_____

e. help_____   *j.* work_____

Grammar Task Card: Adjectives 4

1. Write two adjectives to describe each of these nouns.

train   mountain   tiger   athlete   parrot

butterfly   house   spider   meal   orange

2. Adjectives of degree—fill in the spaces.

a. fat   fatter   fattest   *e.* steep   _____   _____

b. long   _____   _____   *f.* _____   wider   _____

c. _____   _____   brightest   *g.* _____   _____   happiest

d. dirty   _____   _____   *h.* good   _____   _____

3. Write the antonyms of these words.

happy   old   stale   fast   long   narrow   straight

sour   light   kind   clean   strong   small   low

Grammar Task Card: Pronouns

1

1. Put in the correct pronoun: *she*, *her*, or *hers*.

   a. Give _____ things back to _____.

   b. _____ and I will go shopping tomorrow.

   c. If this book is _____, give it to _____.

   d. _____ was the last meal to be served.

   e. _____ put her hands under _____ chin.

2. Don't confuse *their* and *there*. (Example: They will put on <u>their</u> shoes. They will stand <u>there</u> by the wall.)

   a. Did you see _____ paintings?

   b. Can you leave my bike _____ in the bike rack?

   c. Stand _____ and don't move!

   d. The girls put on _____ hats and _____ socks and shoes.

   e. Everyone _____ fell asleep in _____ chairs.

Grammar Task Card: Pronouns

2

1. The pronouns are missing from these sentences. Rewrite the sentences, adding in the pronouns.

   a. Jack left _____ bag on the bus.

   b. The boys put all _____ toys away in _____ toy box.

   c. Did _____ see the zebras at the zoo?

   d. Wait for _____ and _____ can go together.

   e. "Give _____ back _____ ball, please," _____ said.

2. Begin these questions with *who*, *which*, *what*, or *whose*.

   a. _____ will help me make a clay pot?

   b. _____ boy is the fastest runner?

   c. _____ would you like for dinner?

   d. _____ are cheaper, the apples or the oranges?

   e. _____ book is this?

Grammar Task Card: Pronouns 3

1. Add a possessive pronoun.

a. The cat licks _____ paws.

b. I wash _____ face and _____ hands.

c. Did you give it to _____ brother?

d. The pet mouse is _____.

e. Do you know _____ name?

f. I don't know if it is _____.

2. Rewrite the sentences using the correct pronoun.

a. He is (my, mine) lifelong friend.

b. Did you see (their, them)?

c. Do you want (we, us) to come with (you, yours)?

d. This parrot is (him, his), but he is giving it to (I, me).

e. This is (me, my) hat. I want to see (its, his).

f. (They, Them) will play a game of baseball.

g. Please buy tickets for Danika and (I, me).

Grammar Task Card: Pronouns 4

1. Use these pronouns in sentences.

him	our	they	us
your	we	her	mine

2. What nouns do the underlined pronouns replace?

a. "Show me <u>your</u> African drum, Jake," said Andrew.

b. Mom said, "Bring <u>me</u> your clothes to wash."

c. "Show me <u>your</u> homework," the teacher said to the class.

d. Jane looked at the painting and said, "<u>It</u> is wonderful!"

e. "Will you take <u>my</u> photo?" Jen asked Raj.

f. Ryan said to Alex, "<u>I</u> will phone you on Sunday."

g. "<u>We</u> can go home now, Ella," said Jacob.

Grammar Task Card: Verbs

1

1. Word Trap: *did* or *done*? Fill in the blanks.

(Tip: *Done* always needs a helper—I <u>did</u> my work. I <u>have done</u> my work.)

    a. We _____ our homework.
    e. The artist _____ some painting.

    b. They have _____ a good job.
    f. Have you _____ all your chores?

    c. I have not _____ anything wrong.
    g. We knew he had _____ it.

    d. _____ you see the brown owl?
    h. Has she _____ her math?

Write your own sentences using *did* and *done*.

2. Word Trap: *went* or *gone*? Fill in the blanks.

(Tip: *Gone* always needs a helper—She <u>went</u> to school. She <u>has gone</u> to school.)

    a. He _____ to the river.
    e. I _____ to see Uncle Harry.

    b. They have _____ for a swim.
    f. Has he _____ yet?

    c. Has she _____ with them?
    g. We _____ home early.

    d. Tom _____ by car.
    h. Where have they _____?

Write your own sentences using *went* and *gone*.

Grammar Task Card: Verbs

2

1. Word Trap: *saw* or *seen*? Fill in the blanks.

(Tip: *Seen* always need a helper—They <u>saw</u> the movie. They <u>have seen</u> the movie.)

    a. I _____ you climbing that tree.
    e. You _____ the match, didn't you?

    b. Have you _____ my kitten?
    f. We _____ where you lived.

    c. He _____ me on the bus.
    g. Has he _____ your new bike?

    d. She has _____ the movie twice.
    h. I don't know who you _____.

Write your own sentences using *saw* and *seen*.

2. List only the verbs.

throw	plastic	stir	listen	ugly	chew	shabby	choose
gold	speak	has	seize	during	down	draw	construct

Well

Grammar Task Card: Verbs

3

1. Rewrite these sentences in the past tense.

    a. Sue and Lynn will go for a walk on Sunday.

    b. The boys eat cashew nuts and drink lemonade.

    c. We think his painting is the best one of all.

    d. They stand when the teacher comes in.

2. Write these negative verbs as contractions.

a. did not	*d.* cannot	*g.* will not	*j.* have not
b. could not	*e.* is not	*h.* was not	*k.* do not
c. has not	*f.* would not	*i.* are not	*l.* were not

3. Add the correct suffix: *–ing* or *–ed*.

One day, a boy and his dog were walk_____ along a mountain path. The boy whistle_____ as he walk_____. The dog follow_____ close at his heels. They had not walk_____ far when the dog spot_____ a lizard. He chase_____ the tiny creature, bark_____. The lizard scurry_____ up a tree. The dog snap_____ at his tail, but he miss_____.

Grammar Task Card: Verbs

4

1. Add an interesting verb to each subject.

a. birds _____	*d.* fireflies _____	*g.* trucks _____
b. sirens_____	*e.* water _____	*h.* horses _____
c. camels _____	*f.* hens _____	*i.* people _____

2. Sort these verbs into "doing" verbs and "saying" verbs.

shout	tumble	roar	skip	wait	giggle
argue	pinch	scream	roll	scold	ride

3. Write these pronouns and verbs as contractions.

a. she will	*d.* he is	*g.* they are	*j.* we would
b. they have	*e.* we are	*h.* he would	*k.* I am
c. you are	*f.* I would	*i.* she has	*l.* we will

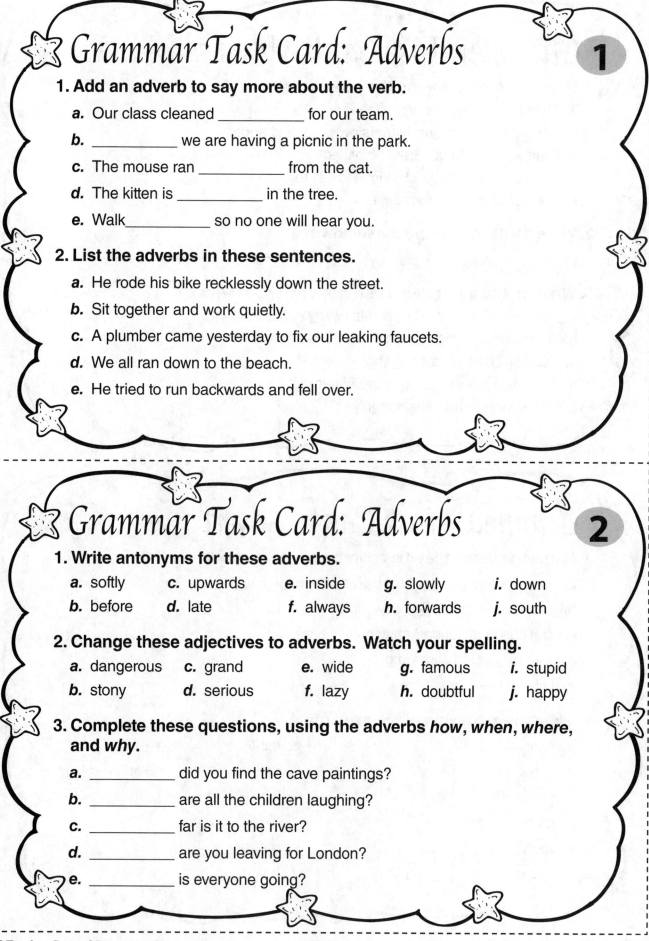

Grammar Task Card: Adverbs

1. 1. **Add an adverb to say more about the verb.**

   a. Our class cleaned _____ for our team.

   b. _____ we are having a picnic in the park.

   c. The mouse ran _____ from the cat.

   d. The kitten is _____ in the tree.

   e. Walk_____ so no one will hear you.

2. **List the adverbs in these sentences.**

   a. He rode his bike recklessly down the street.

   b. Sit together and work quietly.

   c. A plumber came yesterday to fix our leaking faucets.

   d. We all ran down to the beach.

   e. He tried to run backwards and fell over.

Grammar Task Card: Adverbs

2. 1. **Write antonyms for these adverbs.**

   a. softly   *c.* upwards   *e.* inside   *g.* slowly   *i.* down
   b. before   *d.* late   *f.* always   *h.* forwards   *j.* south

2. **Change these adjectives to adverbs. Watch your spelling.**

   a. dangerous   *c.* grand   *e.* wide   *g.* famous   *i.* stupid
   b. stony   *d.* serious   *f.* lazy   *h.* doubtful   *j.* happy

3. **Complete these questions, using the adverbs *how*, *when*, *where*, and *why*.**

   a. _____ did you find the cave paintings?

   b. _____ are all the children laughing?

   c. _____ far is it to the river?

   d. _____ are you leaving for London?

   e. _____ is everyone going?

Grammar Task Card: Adverbs

3

1. Use the correct word in the parentheses.

   a. Rain fell (heavy, heavily) on the roof.

   b. Tired now, Ken swam (slow, slowly) back to shore.

   c. Please don't shout. Speak (soft, softly).

   d. The coach spoke (kind, kindly) to her team.

   e. You acted (foolish, foolishly).

2. Write sentences using these adverbs.

there   often   sleepily   sometimes   sternly

3. What do the adverbs tell us—*how*, *when*, or *where*?

   a. The flower seller opens her stall <u>early</u> in the morning.

   b. She listened <u>patiently</u> to her brother's explanation.

   c. I couldn't find my cat <u>anywhere</u>.

   d. <u>Tomorrow</u> we are going to the rain forest.

   e. The fox eyed the hens <u>hungrily</u>.

Grammar Task Card: Adverbs

4

1. Name the verbs that the adverb say more about.

   a. He crept <u>forward slowly</u> to the mouth of the cave.

   b. The kite landed <u>upside down</u> in a tree.

   c. The children laughed <u>excitedly</u>.

   d. You go <u>now</u>. I'll come <u>later</u>.

   e. I buy the newspaper <u>daily</u>.

2. Write the antonyms of these words.

   a. happily   *g.* tightly

   b. outside   *h.* painfully

   c. gracefully   *i.* lightly

   d. quickly   *j.* kindly

   e. warmly   *k.* messily

   f. above   *l.* before

Grammar Task Card: Phrases

1

1. Draw the following. The phrases will help you.

a. a cat on a chair

b. a dog with a bone

c. a bike against a fence

d. a white shirt with red stripes

e. a girl with long hair

f. a man beside his truck

g. a plane above the clouds

h. a jar of peanut butter

2. Complete the phrases.

a. We all laughed at _____.

b. The ball rolled under _____.

c. He came to school without _____.

d. We all had hats except _____.

e. Please don't go near _____.

Grammar Task Card: Phrases

2

1. Circle the phrases in these sentences.

a. My shoes are under the bed.

b. After dinner, I wash the dishes.

c. It rained during the night.

d. A snake slithered behind the shed.

e. The marbles in that bag belong to Adam.

2. The adjectival phrases are underlined. To which nouns do they refer?

a. The lighthouse <u>on the coast</u> warns ships of danger.

b. The animal <u>with the long neck</u> is a giraffe.

c. In autumn, the leaves <u>of the trees</u> turn golden yellow.

d. The path <u>through the forest</u> is damp and shady.

e. I have a new blue shirt <u>with long sleeves</u>.

Grammar Task Card: Phrases

3

1. Add an adjectival phrase.

a. The dog _____ barked at the lizard.

b. The bike _____ belongs to Thomas.

c. The cup _____ has a chipped handle.

d. Put the vase _____ in the center of the table.

e. The trees _____ are losing their leaves.

2. The adverbial phrases are underlined. Do they tell us *how*, *when*, or *why*?

a. Let's play soccer <u>in the backyard</u>.

b. You may read together <u>for ten minutes</u>.

c. <u>With a frightened cry</u>, the girl ran away.

d. I will wait <u>for you</u>.

e. <u>Last night</u>, the moon was full.

Grammar Task Card: Prepositions

1

1. Use these prepositions in sentences.

| between | past | around | after |
| off | of | for | |

2. Use prepositions to fill in the blanks.

a. Did you look _____ the cupboard?

b. Dad bought a packet _____ fish sinkers.

c. She has a pimple _____ the tip _____ her nose.

d. My dog likes to walk _____ me.

e. _____ night, owls search _____ food.

Grammar Task Card: Sentences

1. Rewrite only the sentences and punctuate them.

    a. cats stalk birds

    b. during the match

    c. the man stroked his beard

    d. with his back to the wall

    e. vegetables in my garden

    f. we sang around the piano

    g. wild horses galloped by the farm

    h. in five minutes or so

    i. they go camping by the lake

    j. was there someone at the door

2. Write sentences around these ideas.

    a. truck   haul

    b. stage   dance

    c. cage   escape

    d. crowd   roar

    e. boat   capsize

    f. mountain   climb

3. Think about a topic you know a lot about (Examples: a game, a toy, an animal). Write five questions about your topic to ask your classmates. You should also write the answers to your questions using sentences.

Grammar Task Card: Sentences

1. Write two facts and two opinions (your own) about these subjects.

    a. potato chips

    b. roses

    c. computer games

    d. your school

    e. baseball

    f. books

2. Imagine what is happening in these exclamations. Choose five and draw a quick drawing for each.

    a. Oh, no! Not again!

    b. Look out! Stand back!

    c. Surprise!

    d. How could you do such a thing!

    e. Back off!

    f. That's not fair!

    g. What a mess!

    h. That is amazing!

    i. Come on! Hurry!

    j. You're in trouble!

Grammar Task Card: Sentences 3

1. **Join the two sentences to make a compound sentence. Use the conjunctions *and*, *but*, or *so*.**

   a. Jayne likes pears.   Con likes plums.
   b. It is late.   I must leave.
   c. I ate a cookie.   I drank a glass of milk.
   d. The lightning flashed.   The thunder crashed.
   e. I would come with you.   I don't have time.
   f. He shouted loudly.   No one heard him.

2. **Join the predicates to their correct subjects.**

   a. The boys in the go-kart   dangled in its web.
   b. My yellow kite   played chess.
   c. After dinner, Mandy and I   rushed down the hill.
   d. A large black spider   was nestled at the foot of the mountain.
   e. A tiny village   hit the top of the tree.

Grammar Task Card: Sentences 4

1. **Write a statement and a question about each subject.**

   a. a tiny hut   *d.* the boy from Japan
   b. an African drum   *e.* my longtime friend
   c. a dark, damp cave   *f.* a lost kitten

2. **What are the subjects of these sentences?**

   a. Cyclones bring high winds and heavy rain.
   b. At our school, all students wear a school uniform.
   c. After three hours, the top-ranked tennis player finally won his match.
   d. By the end of the week, all homework must be complete.
   e. You have worked very hard.

3. **Punctuate this dialogue.**

   Can I help you sir asked the salesman

   Yes please said Mr Dobbs I would like some rechargeable batteries

   Of course sir said the salesman what size do you need

TARGETING GRAMMAR

WORD BANKS

200

©Teacher Created Resources, Inc.

WORD BANKS
Antonyms
Opposites

ADJECTIVES

awake	*asleep*
black	*white*
bright	*dull*
clean	*dirty*
cold	*hot*
dear	*cheap/inexpensive*
expensive	*cheap*
far	*near*
fast	*slow*
fat	*thin*
fat	*lean*
fresh	*stale*
full	*empty*
great	*small*
high	*low*
ill	*well*
kind	*unkind*
light	*dark*
light	*heavy*
little	*big*
long	*short*
old	*new*
old	*young*
right	*wrong*
right	*left*
sad	*happy*
small	*large*
smooth	*rough*
smooth	*coarse*
soft	*hard*
soft	*loud*
top	*bottom*
ugly	*beautiful*
wet	*dry*
wide	*narrow*
wild	*tame*

VERBS

come	*go*	open	*close*
ebb	*flow*	sleep	*wake*
open	*shut*	stand	*sit*
sink	*float*	stop	*go*
throw	*catch*	win	*lose*

NOUNS

day	*night*	dawn	*dusk*
love	*hate*	friend	*foe/enemy*
morning	*night*	life	*death*

ADVERBS

late	*early*	now	*then*
sooner	*later*	often	*seldom*

PREPOSITIONS

above	*below*	behind	*ahead*
after	*before*	in	*out*
off	*on*	over	*under*
up	*down*	with	*without*

a brood of chickens

a business of ferrets

a cete of badgers

a cloud of flies

a clowder of cats

a clutch of eggs

a flock of birds

a gaggle of geese

a herd of buffalo

a herd of elephants

a litter of cubs

a mob of cattle

a murder of crows

a pack of dogs

a rake of colts

a shoal of fish

a shrewdness of apes

a siege of herons

a skulk of foxes

a sloth of bears

a swarm of bees

an army of frogs

a bevy of quail

a convoy of trucks

a covey of partridges

an exaltation of larks

a flock of sheep

a kindle of kittens

a leap of leopards

a mob of kangaroos

a pack of wolves

a parliament of owls

a pod of whales

a pride of lions

a rafter of turkeys

a school of porpoises

a smack of jellyfish

a string of racehorses

a team of horses

a tiding of magpies

a troop of monkeys

a warren of rabbits

a wedge of swans

afternoon	daytime	footbridge/footloose
anthill	dipstick	footpath/footprint
armchair	doorbell	fullback
backside	doorknob	gentleman
bandstand	doorstep	goalkeeper
barnyard	doorstop	godmother/godfather
baseball	doorway	grandmother/grandfather
basketball	downhearted	grandstand
bathroom	downhill	grapefruit
bedroom/bedtime	downstairs	grapevine
bellboy	downstream	halfback
birthday	downtown	handbag
blackboard	downtrodden	handheld
bookcase	drainpipe	handlebar
bookends	driveway	handmade
bookmark	eggplant	handstand
bridegroom	eggshell	haystack
broomstick	eyebrow	headlight
bulldozer	eyelash	heartbeat/heartfelt
bull's-eye	eyeliner	herself/himself
buttercup	fail-safe	hillside
buttermilk	fairway	homeland
butterscotch	fairytale	homesick
cardboard	farmland	homestead
carthorse	farmyard	horseback/horseplay
cartwheel	fingernail	horsehair/horseshoe
catfish	fireball/firefly	hornpipe
cornflakes	firelight/fireplace	houseboat
cowboy/cowgirl	fireman/firestorm	household
daybreak	fireproof	inland/inlet
daydream	foolhardy	inside
daylight	football/footman	jumpstart

junkyard

kickboxer

landslide/landline

leeway

lifeline/lifetime

lighthouse

lightweight

lunchbox

manhole

manpower

matchbox

matchstick

merry-go-round

milkman

milkshake

moonlight/moonbeam

mothballs

mudpie

nevermore

nickname

nightdress

nightfall

nighttime

nursemaid

offside

outpost

outside

overall

overeat

overleaf

overstay

overtime

paperweight

pathway

penknife

pickpocket

pigsty

pinwheel

playtime/playhouse

policeman

popcorn

porthole

postcard

postman

pothole

quarterback

quarter-time

railway/railroad

rainbow/raindrops

raincoat

rosebud

sandbag

sandcastle

scarecrow

shockproof

shoelace/shoestring

showtime

skylight

slipstream/slipway

snowball/snowflake

snowman

softball

starlight/starburst

steamroller

stopwatch

sunbeam/sunburst

sunlight/sunshine

tablecloth

teapot

telltale

timeline

timepiece

toenail

toothpaste/toothbrush

topside

towbar

toyshop

washstand

watchmaker

waterbed/watermelon

watercolor/waterway

watercourse/waterproof

waterfront/watercress

waterhole/watertight

watermark/waterfall

waterworks

waxworks

weekend/weekday

whirlwind

windmill

witchcraft

WORD BANKS

Gender refers to whether something is *male*, *female*, or *neither (neuter)*. Pronouns *he, his, him, she, her, hers, it,* and *its* show the gender of someone or something in English. Some suffixes show whether something is male or female. Nowadays these suffixes tend not to be used with people, as they may be considered to be sexist (Examples: actor, actress; hero, heroine).

boar, sow	actor, actress
bull, cow	author
cob, swan	aviator
drake, duck	baron, baroness
drone, bee	count, countess
fox, vixen	duke, duchess
gander, goose	emperor, empress
gentleman, lady	hero, heroine
lion, lioness	king, queen
man, woman	lord, lady
ram, ewe	poet
rooster, hen	prince, princess
stag (or buck), doe	sir, dame
stallion, mare	sir, madam
steer, heifer	uncle, aunt
tiger, tigress	waiter, waitress

acts/ax	braise/brays	dear/deer
ail/ale	brake/break	dew/due
air/heir	bread/bred	die/dye
aisle/isle/I'll	brews/bruise	died/dyed
allowed/aloud	bridal/bridle	dies/dyes
alter/altar	buy/by/bye	doe/dough
arc/ark	cannon/canon	draft/draught
ascent/assent	canvas/canvass	dying/dyeing
ate/eight	capital/capitol	earn/urn
aunt/ant	carrot/carat	ewe/you/yew
bail/bale	cast/caste	ewes/use
bald/bawled	cede/seed	eye/I
bare/bear	ceiling/sealing	eyelet/islet
barren/baron	cellar/seller	faint/feint
base/bass	cent/scent/sent	fair/fare
be/bee	cents/scents/sense	farther/father
beach/beech	cereal/serial	fate/fete
been/bean	cheap/cheep	feat/feet
beer/bier	chews/choose	find/fined
bell/belle	choral/coral	fir/fur
berry/bury	cite/sight/site	flea/flee
birth/berth	clause/claws	flew/flu/flue
blew/blue	coarse/course	flow/floe
boar/bore	colonel/kernel	flower/flour
board/bored	core/corps	for/fore/four
boarder/border	council/counsel	foul/fowl
bold/bowled	creak/creek	frays/phrase
born/borne	crews/cruise	gait/gate
bough/bow	cue/queue	genes/jeans
bow/beau	currant/current	gild/guild
boy/buoy	cygnet/signet	gored/gourd
braid/brayed	days/daze	gorilla/guerilla

grate/great

grater/greater

groan/grown

guest/guessed

hail/hale

hanger/hangar

hart/heart

heal/heel/he'll

hear/here

heard/herd

hears/here's

hew/hue

higher/hire

him/hymn

ho/hoe

hoard/horde

hoarse/horse

hose/hoes

hole/whole

holy/wholly

hour/our

idle/idol

in/inn

jam/jamb

knead/need/kneed

knew/new

knight/night

knot/not

know/no

knows/nose

lacks/lax

lain/lane

laps/lapse

lead/led

leak/leek

lessen/lesson

liar/lyre

lightening/lightning

links/lynx

load/lode

loan/lone

made/maid

main/mane

maize/maze

mall/maul

manner/manor

mantel/mantle

mare/mayor

marshal/martial

meat/meet/mete

medal/meddle

metal/mettle

might/mite

mined/mind

miner/minor

missed/mist

moan/mown

moat/mote

mode/mowed

more/moor

morn/mourn

morning/mourning

muscle/mussel

mustard/mustered

nay/neigh

none/nun

ode/owed

one/won

or/oar/ore

paced/paste

packed/pact

pail/pale

pain/pane

pair/pare/pear

passed/past

patience/patients

peace/piece

peak/peek

peer/pier

pedal/peddle

poor/pore

WORD BANKS Prefixes
change word meaning

a– on, in, into, to	**ab–** off, away, from	**ad–** direction, addition	**after–** afterwards	**ante–** before in space/time
aboard	abduct	adjacent	afterburner	antebellum
about	abhor	adjourn	afterimage	antecedent
adrift	abnormal	adjudicate	afterlife	antechamber
afoot	abort	adjust	aftermath	antedated
alight	absent	admire	afternoon	antelope
along	absolute	admit	aftershave	antemeridian
aloud	absolve	advance	aftershock	antemundane
among	absorb	advantage	aftertaste	antenatal
anew	abstain	adversity	afterthought	anterior
away	abstract	advocate	afterwards	anteroom

anti– against, opposite of	**arch–** first, chief	**auto–** self	**bene–** well	**bi–** two
antibiotic	archfiend	autobiography	benediction	bicentenary
anticlimax	archrival	autocrat	benedictory	bicycle
anticlockwise	archvillain	autocue	benefaction	biennial
antidote	archangel	autograph	benefactor	bifocal
antifreeze	archbishop	autoharp	benefice	bilingual
antigovernment	archdeacon	automatic	beneficial	binoculars
antioxidant	archduchess	automaton	beneficiary	biped
antiperspirant	archduke	automobile	benefit	biplane
antisocial	archenemy	autopilot	benevolence	bipolar
antiviral	archetype	autosuggestion	benevolent	bisect

circum– round	**co–** association/action	**com–** with, jointly	**con–** with, jointly, in combination	**contra–** opposite/opposing
circumference	coagulate	combination	concentrate	contraband
circumfluent	coaxial	combine	condition	contrabass
circumlocutory	codependence	combustion	confide	contraception
circumnavigate	coerce	commence	congenial	contraceptive
circumscribe	coexist	commute	congratulate	contradict
circumspect	cohabit	complacent	connect	contralto
circumstance	cohesive	complain	consent	contravene
circumstantial	coincidence	complete	consider	
circumstantiate	cooperate	compose	converge	
circumvent	coordinate	compute	convince	

WORD BANKS Prefixes
change word meaning

counter *contrary to*	**de–** *separation, negation, reversal*	**di–** *through, between, across, by*	**dis–** *away, apart, reversing effect*	**down–** *downwards*
counteract counterattack counterbalance counterintelligence countermand counteroffensive counterpart countersign countersink counterweight	debrief decay decide decompose deduct delay depend destroy determine develop	digest digress dilate dilute dimension direct divergent divert divest divulge	disagree disappear disband discard discourage discover dislocate disobey displace dissolve	downfall downgrade downhearted downhill downpipe downpour downstairs downstream downtown downtrodden

dys– *difficulty, poor condition*	**e–** *variant of ex–*	**en–** *in, into*	**epi–** *near, to, against, above, after, in addition to*	**eu–** *good, well*
dysentery dysfunctional dysgenic dyslexia dyspepsia dysphasia dysphonic dysphoria dysplasia	elaborate electric emerge enormous eradicate erase erect evacuate evaluate evolve	enable enchant encircle encourage encroach enforce engulf enlighten enliven entreat	epicenter epicure epidemic epidermis epigram epilogue episode epitaph epithet epitome	eucalyptus Eucharist euchre eulogy eunuch euphonium eureka eurhythmic Europe euthanasia

ex– *from, out of, utterly, thoroughly*	**extra–** *beyond, outside, besides*	**fore–** *front, ahead of time*	**hyper–** *over, excess, exaggeration*	**hypo–** *under, less, less than*
excavate exclaim exhale explain explore export ex-president exterminate extreme ex-wife	extradite extragalactic extrajudicial extraneous extraordinary extrapolate extrasensory extraterrestrial extraterritorial extravagant	foreboding forecast forefront forego foreground forehead foreshadow foretaste foretell forewarn	hyperactive hyperbole hypermarket hyperphysical hypersensitive hypersonic hyperspace hypertension hyperventilate	hypoactive hypochondriac hypocrite hypocritical hypodermic hypoglycemic hypotenuse hypothermia hypotheses hypothetical

WORD BANKS Prefixes
change word meaning

il– *variant of in–*	im– *variant of in–*	in– *not*	inter– *between*	mis– *mistaken, wrong, negation*
illegal illegible illegitimate illicit illiterate illogical ill-timed ill-treat illuminate illustrious	imbalance immature immeasurable immortal immovable impassable impatient impersonal impossible improbable	inaccurate inanimate inappropriate inarticulate incredible inexcusable inexplicable informal invincible invisible	interact interfere interject intermingle international Internet interrupt interschool intersect interstate	misbehave miscalculate misfortune mishap misjudge misplace mispronounce misrepresent mistrust misuse

over– *above, beyond*	para– *beyond, near, beside, amiss*	peri– *around, about, beyond*	post– *behind, after*	pre– *before, prior to*
overall overbearing overboard overdose overdue overhead overjoyed overlook overrate overtake	parachute paradox paragon paragraph parallel paramedic paramount paranormal paraphernalia paraphrase	perilous perimeter periodic peripatetic peripheral periphery periphrastic periscope peristyle periwinkle	postdate posterity postgraduate posthumous postmortem postnatal postpone postposition postscript postwar	precaution precede precooked predict prefix prehistoric prejudge prelude premonition presuppose

pro– *for, before, in favor of*	re– *back, again, reversal*	retro– *backwards in space and time*	se– *setting apart, taking away*	semi– *half*
probation proceed profound prognosis program progress prohibit prologue promote pronounce	refer regain relate relight remake remit replay restore resume return	retroactive retrocede retroflex retrograde retrogressive retro-rocket retrorse retrospect retrospective retroversion	secede secluded secrete secure security seduce select semester sequence serene	semicircle semicolon semiconscious semidesert semidetached semifinal semiprecious semiquaver semiskilled semitone

WORD BANKS Prefixes
change word meaning

sub– *under, not quite*	super– *above, superior*	sym– *variant of syn–*	syn– *association (like co–)*	trans– *across, beyond*
subcontract subheading submerge subsonic substandard substitute subterranean subtitle subtropical subway	supercharged superimpose superintendent supermarket supernatural supersede superstar superstructure super-tanker supervise	symbol symbolic symmetrical symmetry sympathize sympathy symphony symphysis symposium symptom	synagogue synapsis synchronize synchronous syndicate syndrome synergy syntax synthesis synthesize	transcontinental transfer transform translate translucent transmit transparent transport transpose transverse
tri– *three*	ultra– *beyond in space and time*	un– *not, opposite to, reversal of state*	under– *below—place or situation*	up– *upwards*
triangle triceps tricolor tricycle triennial trihedron trilogy trimaran triplets tripod	ultrasensitive ultraconservative ultracritical ultrafilter ultraloyal ultramarine ultraradical ultrasonic ultrasound ultraviolet	unarmed unbeatable unbend unclean undesirable unfold untimely untraceable untruth unusual	underclothes underdog underestimate undergrowth underline undermine underneath undernourished undervalue underweight	update upgrade upheaval uphill uplifted upright upscale upstage upstart upstream

Adjective-forming suffixes

–al	–ive	–ish	–ic	–ent
casual	active	babyish	bombastic	deficient
coastal	attentive	brownish	comic	dependent
lethal	attractive	devilish	domestic	despondent
local	compulsive	foolish	dramatic	efficient
minimal	effective	impish	idiotic	eloquent
occasional	festive	oldish	optimistic	insolent
personal	impulsive	peckish	pessimistic	proficient
regional	negative	Spanish	rustic	prominent
thermal	positive	stylish	static	reverent
usual	sensitive	sweetish	toxic	transient

–ful	–less	–some	–able	–ible
careful	breathless	awesome	agreeable	admissible
cheerful	defenseless	bothersome	changeable	divisible
colorful	fearless	cumbersome	comfortable	edible
doubtful	leaderless	flavorsome	desirable	horrible
fanciful	merciless	gruesome	fashionable	in/visible
helpful	motherless	handsome	miserable	in/credible
peaceful	numberless	loathsome	reasonable	possible
powerful	relentless	meddlesome	reliable	responsible
thoughtful	sleepless	tiresome	untraceable	sensible
truthful	timeless	wearisome	workable	terrible

–er –est _comparative/superlative_		–ial	–ous	–ious	–y
calmer	calmest	beneficial	adventurous	delicious	fizzy
faster	fastest	commercial	continuous	devious	funny
happier	happiest	differential	famous	fallacious	greasy
higher	highest	influential	generous	gracious	greedy
hotter	hottest	official	jealous	illustrious	hungry
longer	longest	partial	mountainous	impervious	risky
older	oldest	preferential	nervous	malicious	speedy
slower	slowest	sequential	perilous	officious	sunny
thicker	thickest	superficial	pompous	precious	tasty
thinner	thinnest	territorial	venomous	spacious	tricky

WORD BANKS Suffixes
change word grammar

Noun-forming suffixes

–acy	–ant	–ary, –ory, –ery	–ance	–ence
accuracy	assistant	cemetery	abundance	competence
bureaucracy	attendant	diary	accordance	conference
conspiracy	combatant	dispensary	circumstance	correspondence
democracy	commandant	documentary	distance	dependence
fallacy	confidant	eatery	disturbance	eloquence
intimacy	consonant	factory	elegance	experience
legacy	dependant	infirmary	entrance	inference
lunacy	pedant	mortuary	nuisance	innocence
piracy	pendant	refectory	performance	persistence
privacy	servant	seminary	reluctance	prudence

–ium	–er	–ism	–ist	–ice
aquarium	announcer	communism	dentist	accomplice
auditorium	baker	escapism	egotist	apprentice
conservatorium	builder	fanaticism	exhibitionist	armistice
millennium	buyer	fatalism	extremist	cornice
planetarium	dancer	favoritism	guitarist	in/justice
podium	driver	idealism	opportunist	novice
premium	photographer	impressionism	racist	police
solarium	player	racism	sadist	practice
stadium	teacher	rheumatism	soloist	prejudice
terrarium	trader	unionism	violinist	service

–cle	–hood	–itis	–ion	–tion
debacle	adulthood	appendicitis	apprehension	collection
icicle	babyhood	arthritis	conclusion	competition
manacle	brotherhood	bronchitis	decision	destination
monocle	childhood	dermatitis	derision	education
oracle	falsehood	fibrositis	illusion	pollution
particle	fatherhood	laryngitis	impression	explanation
pinnacle	motherhood	meningitis	occasion	illustration
receptacle	parenthood	peritonitis	opinion	instruction
spectacle	priesthood	sinusitis	pension	invitation
tentacle	sainthood	tonsillitis	question	recreation

WORD BANKS Suffixes
change word grammar

Noun-forming suffixes *(cont.)*

–ment	–ness	–ship	–ity	–ian
amazement	awkwardness	censorship	authenticity	electrician
amusement	carelessness	companionship	complicity	guardian
appointment	darkness	craftsmanship	domesticity	Italian
engagement	laziness	fellowship	electricity	mathematician
entertainment	madness	friendship	facility	musician
management	selfishness	horsemanship	familiarity	pediatrician
movement	softness	leadership	mediocrity	pedestrian
predicament	sweetness	partnership	security	politician
refreshment	tenderness	relationship	similarity	technician
wonderment	uneasiness	scholarship	toxicity	vegetarian

–age	–ent, –ee	–le	–or	–ette
blockage	agent	battle	actor	cigarette
bondage	antecedent	bubble	author	dinette
breakage	devotee	bundle	conductor	diskette
damage	employee	candle	contractor	etiquette
foliage	evacuee	couple	doctor	kitchenette
hostage	precedent	kettle	mentor	marionette
leakage	president	pimple	sailor	rosette
marriage	refugee	puzzle	sculptor	silhouette
postage	respondent	rifle	senator	suffragette
storage	student	saddle	visitor	usherette

Adverb-forming suffixes

–ly	–ward/s	–wise	–way/s
busily	afterward	anticlockwise	always
daily	backwards	clockwise	anyway
gladly	downwards	crosswise	away
honestly	forwards	lengthwise	everyway
lately	homeward	likewise	lengthways
presently	inwards	moneywise	longways
quietly	outwards	otherwise	sideways
reluctantly	towards	penny-wise	someway
slowly	wayward	timewise	underway
usually	westward	waterwise	

NOUNS

Student Page 1 (page 20)

1. a. Brianna, sister, school, car
   b. friend, ice cream, jelly, custard
   c. horse, hill, pasture, fence

2. Answers will vary.

3. a. eagle
   b. barn
   c. Answers will vary.
   d. Answers will vary.

4. PEOPLE (red): prisoner, singer, dentist; ANIMALS (blue): rabbit, bear, caterpillar; PLACES (yellow): beach, playground, office; THINGS (green): ladder, cloud, statue

5. Answers will vary.

Student Page 2 (page 21)

1. a. bus
   b. book, snakes
   c. brother, skateboard
   d. fly, moth, web
   e. knives, forks, spoons, table

2. a. 3—toddler, milk, cookie
   b. 1—window
   c. 3—man, desert, camel
   d. 2—hill, school
   e. 3—teacher, books, story

3. Answers will vary.

Student Page 3 (page 22)

1. Answers will vary.

2. Brian has a pen pal who lives in France. His name is Jacques. Jacques lives in the city of Paris beside the River Seine. Brian and Jacques both love to play soccer. One day Jacques would like to visit Brian in Australia.

3. Answers will vary.

Student Page 4 (page 23)

1. singular: hen, book, coat, carrot, tub; plural: cards, bikes, flies, peaches, coyotes

2. a. bells   f. pencils
   b. cakes   g. kites
   c. boxes   h. flowers
   d. branches   i. calves
   e. socks   j. babies

3. child—children; goose—geese; mouse—mice; foot—feet; man—men

Student Page 5 (page 24)

1. Suggested answers:
   a. sunlight   f. stopwatch
   b. downstairs or downhill g. raindrops
   c. manhole   h. dragonfly
   d. baseball   i. bookcase
   e. anthill   j. eggshell

2. tablecloth, toothpaste, postcard, football, farmyard, matchbox

3. Sentences will vary.

Student Page 6 (page 25)

T	B	R	A	L	P	W	Z	Y	E
A	K	I	T	T	E	N	S	N	T
S	A	C	R	D	L	I	O	N	S
F	N	H	Y	B	E	R	S	Q	K
B	G	I	M	U	P	D	H	A	W
P	A	C	L	S	H	O	E	T	O
G	R	K	B	P	A	M	E	F	L
R	O	E	J	R	N	C	P	R	V
U	O	N	X	G	T	V	Y	T	E
B	S	S	U	M	S	B	E	E	S

1. a. kittens   e. kangaroos
   b. elephants   f. sheep
   c. chickens   g. bees
   d. wolves   h. lions

2. crowd of people, pod of whales, school of fish, school of porpoises, flock of seagulls, pod of whales

3. Drawings will vary.

Student Page 7 (page 26)

1. a. It is Danielle's horse.
   b. It is Mr. Tan's car.
   c. It is a spider's web.
   d. They are the dinosaur's bones.
   e. They are the birds' nests.
   f. They are the men's golf balls.

2. a. builder   d. women
   b. owls   e. friend
   c. farmer   f. Emily

3. Answers will vary.

Student Page 8 (page 27)

1. a. Racing   d. Stargazing
   b. kickboxing   e. Pruning
   c. birdwatching

2. a. Reading is my favorite pastime.
   b. You will need special boots to go rock climbing.

c. Mom put seasoning in the meat stew.
   d. Origami is the art of paper folding.
   e. Tom has a large album for stamp collecting.

3. a. Parking   d. knitting
   b. Playing   e. lighting
   c. fencing

Student Page 9 (page 28)
Answers will vary.

Student Page 10 (page 29)

1. a. teacher   d. goodness
   b. movement   e. builder
   c. softness   f. wonderment

2. a. greatness
   b. player
   c. entertainment or entertainer
   d. banker
   e. amusement
   f. kindness
   g. apartment
   h. fairness
   i. photographer

3. a. darkness   d. gentleness
   b. appointment   e. drummer
   c. refreshments

4. Answers will vary.

Student Page 11 (page 31)

1. Once there was a wild horse. It was snowy white with a long flowing mane. The horse could sometimes be seen in the late afternoon, just before the sun went down. Then it would disappear into a dark, rocky cave. One day, an adventurer who had been walking in the hills was looking for a cave where he might sleep for the night. Behind a large shelf of rock, he found a small cave. It was the cave where the white horse lived. He went inside. He stopped with a gasp at the sight before him. Rays of light, streaming from a hole in the cave roof, fell upon the white horse. It shone like silver in the soft light.

2. Answers will vary.

3. Answers will vary.

Student Page 12 (page 32)

1. a. D I   c. D I
   b. D D   d. D D

ANSWER KEY

2. a. A sleepy, blue-tongue lizard; the warm, brown rocks
   b. An old and wise woman; the bean seeds
   c. the fresh strawberries; a green plastic basket
   d. The frightened horse; the wire fence
   e. a chocolate Easter egg

3. a. a dream   i. an answer
   b. an oven   j. a parrot
   c. a yacht   k. a piano
   d. an axe   l. an avocado
   e. an ostrich   m. a potato
   f. a quest   n. an hour
   g. an iron   o. an inning
   h. an island   p. a pumpkin

Assessment—Nouns (pages 33 and 34)

1. a. quiet   d. pretty
   b. going   e. tall
   c. fast   f. angry

2. James, Byron, clubhouse, Byron's, garden, boards, branch, floor, sheets, walls, roof

3. a. clubhouse, garden, boards, branch, floor, sheets, walls, or roof
   b. James or Byron
   c. Byron's
   d. clubhouse

4. Suggestions: daylight, daytime, junkyard, farmyard, lighthouse, playhouse, farmhouse, waterline, backwater, waterside, backside, backyard, playback, sunlight, playtime, lifetime, lifeline, sideline, Sunday, timeline

5. a. buses   d. babies
   b. plates   e. leaves
   c. days

6. a. sweetness   d. greatness
   b. amusement   e. amazement
   c. gardener

7. The colorful clown, the tiny red car, the large circus ring, a huge green umbrella, All the people

8. a. She washed Sunita's dress.
   b. Milk drips from the cat's whiskers.
   c. Isaac cleaned the teachers' cars.
   d. The workers' boots are very muddy.
   e. The fly's wings beat silently.

9. Answers will vary.

ADJECTIVES

Student Page 13 (page 38)

1. Answers will vary.

2. a. pretty   d. old, gray
   b. young, frisky   e. tall, thin
   c. strong

3. a. tired man, heavy box
   b. sorry boy, exciting football game
   c. dark night, long road
   d. happy dog; great big bone
   e. young girl; kind, friendly teacher

Student Page 14 (page 39)

1. Answers will vary.

2. size (green)—tiny, tall, large; shape (blue)—oval, square, round; sound (yellow)—quiet, loud, noisy; feeling (red)—angry, excited, lazy

3. taste—sweet, tangy, juicy, sour; touch—smooth, uneven, soft, hairy; sight—bright, windy, multicolored, pretty

Student Page 15 (page 40)

1. slow, quiet, old, happy, short, heavy, rough, beautiful, high, below

```
S  F  P  T  N  C  J  O  K  R
D  B  B  E  L  O  W  X  L  B
Y  E  G  Y  P  F  Q  I  H  D
U  A  N  V  O  Z  U  V  G  L
N  U  R  A  R  B  I  T  U  P
S  T  Z  E  L  T  E  F  O  K
H  I  G  H  Q  R  T  M  R  L
O  F  A  E  P  O  W  G  J  G
W  U  T  R  Y  H  A  P  P  Y
S  L  O  W  X  S  H  S  A  D
```

2. a. dirty; b. bottom; c. last; d. full; e. fast; f. dry

3. a. empty/full; b. clean/dirty; c. fast/slow; d. top/bottom

Student Page 16 (page 41)

1. a. dancing shoes
   b. an exciting day/book
   c. swimming suit
   d. falling rocks
   e. an interesting book/day
   f. floating clouds
   g. scented rose
   h. loaded truck
   i. baked pies
   j. polished shoes
   k. mixed nuts
   l. whipped cream

2. Answers will vary.

3. Drawings will vary.

Student Page 17 (page 42)

1. loud, louder, loudest; tall, taller, tallest; fierce, fiercer, fiercest; wet, wetter, wettest; thin, thinner, thinnest; strong, stronger, strongest

2. long, longer, longest; old, older, oldest; sharp, sharper, sharpest; wild, wilder, wildest; soft, softer, softest; brave, braver, bravest

3. a. coldest   d. fastest
   b. warmer   e. larger
   c. older

4. Answers will vary.

Student Page 18 (page 43)

1. a. careful   d. treeless
   b. comfortable   e. adjustable
   c. wonderful

2. a. useful/useless
   b. cheerful/cheerless
   c. shameful/shameless
   d. mindful/mindless

3. Answers will vary.

Student Page 19 (page 44)

1. a. as quiet as a mouse
   b. as busy as a bee
   c. as straight as an arrow
   d. as black as ink
   e. as pale as a ghost

2. a. lamb   e. snow
   b. feather   f. cucumber
   c. dog   g. bat
   d. picture

3. Answers will vary.

4. Answers will vary.

Assessment—Adjectives (pages 45 and 46)

1. a. snowy   d. sore
   b. stinky   e. wet
   c. plastic

2. people—cheerful, smiling, worried, careless; places—foggy, damp, rocky, sandy; things—crunchy, plastic, round, thick

3. a. slim, blonde
   b. rescue, trapped
   c. frightening, haunted
   d. first, solo
   e. gold, sparkling

4. a. low   e. safe
   b. careless   f. rough
   c. ugly   g. empty
   d. big/large   h. wide

5. a. snow   c. lead
   b. picture   d. feather
   Sentences will vary.

6. a. bearable   d. cordless
   b. harmless/harmful   e. passable
   c. handful/handless

7. a. faster   d. stronger
   b. hottest   e. hardest
   c. better

PRONOUNS

Student Page 20 (page 50)

1. a. me   d. I, him
   b. They   e. We, them
   c. her

2. a. She is a great tennis player.
   b. She opened the last birthday present.
   c. It is a heavy wooden one.
   d. They are watching television.

3.

s	m e	r	h e r	p
o	t h e m	l	o d
w e	z f	t h e y
k p	s h e	t n j
t h e i r	b c s
n	y o u r	d n q
u s	n	m a	h e	x
b z h	y	s u w k

4. Drawings will vary.

Student Page 21 (page 51)

1. a. I – S, them – P, me – S
   b. you – S, they – P
   c. He – S, her – S, them – P

2. a. their   d. his
   b. He, his   e. its
   c. mine

3. a. mother
   b. the boys
   c. Sean

d. Debbie and her friend
e. the book

4. Sentences will vary.

Student Page 22 (page 52)

1. a. his   d. our, their
   b. mine   e. your, my
   c. hers

2. a. his   d. their
   b. ours   e. mine
   c. yours

3. Answers will vary.

Student Page 23 (page 54)

1. Answers will vary.

2. Answers will vary.

3. a. Who lost a gold watch?
   b. Whose socks are lying on the floor?
   c. What book are you reading?
   d. Who was playing in the park with you?
   e. Which way is it to the river?

4. a. What   d. Whose
   b. Who   e. whom
   c. Which

Assessment—Pronouns (pages 55 and 56)

1. a. yes   d. no
   b. no   e. yes
   c. yes

2. a. they, it   d. you, us
   b. his, they   e. I, him
   c. her, their

3. Answers will vary.

4. a. the bucket – it
   b. Theo and Jade – they
   c. Rob – he; Aunt Sue – her
   d. the boys – their; Mrs. Wong – her
   e. Chloe – you; Rani – me

5. a. He put his hand under his chin.
   b. Do you always put your toys away?
   c. With their blocks they make a tall tower.
   d. That is his hat. Give it back to him.
   e. Will you come and see me/it/him/her/them/us after school?

6.   Sally looked up and she could see the beach.

   Mr. Green could see why she was sad. Two big tears rolled down her cheeks.

"Sally," he said, "I am not going to keep you. You are free to go. You will be happy here."

   Sally held up her flipper, and Mr. Green gave it a squeeze. Then she went down to the sea. She waved her flipper and dived into the waves.

VERBS

Student Page 24 (page 60)

1. Nouns—horse, sun, school, fork, chair; Verbs—eat, sing, mow, lose, grow

2. a. v, n   d. n
   b. v   e. n, v
   c. n, n

3. Answers will vary.

Student Page 25 (page 61)

1. a. pigs grunt   g. bees buzz
   b. babies cry   h. birds fly
   c. rain falls   i. balls bounce
   d. fish swim   j. horses gallop
   e. wind blows   k. dogs bark
   f. bells ring   l. ants crawl

2. Answers and drawings will vary.

3. a. wash, brush   d. sold, bought
   b. took, ate   e. leaned, lost
   c. bucked, fell

Student Page 26 (page 62)

1. a. squealed   d. called
   b. asked   e. laughed
   c. whispered

2. a. no, yes   d. no, yes
   b. yes, no   e. no, yes
   c. yes, no

3. Answers will vary.

Student Page 27 (page 63)

1. Answers will vary.

Student Page 28 (page 64)

1. a. has, is   f. are, were
   b. has, had   g. are, were
   c. has, had   h. is, was
   d. has, had   i. am, was
   e. is, was   j. has, had

2. a. has   c. is, is
   b. had   d. is, are

3. a. was   c. am
   b. being   d. have

ANSWER KEY

Student Page 29 (page 65)

1. a. is licking d. may be waiting
 b. has been   e. will be playing
 c. can go swimming

2. Answers will vary.

3. can, has, is, was, am, shall, are, have, can, may, will, do, had, have, might, did
 Word: Hi

Student Page 30 (page 66)

1. a. has started d. is playing
 b. have read   e. did win
 c. will go

2. Answers will vary.

3. a. We will <u>not</u> play tennis on Saturday.
 b. The pig is <u>not</u> in its pen.
 c. They have <u>not</u> been to the rodeo.
 d. <u>Do not</u> wait for me!

Student Page 31 (page 67)

1. a. wouldn't—would not
 b. hadn't—had not
 c. didn't—did not
 d. weren't—were not
 e. isn't—is not

2. doesn't – does not, won't – will not, hadn't – had not, weren't – were not, didn't – did not, wouldn't – would not, can't – cannot, wasn't – was not, haven't – have not, aren't – are not, don't – do not, couldn't – could not

3. a. The dogs <u>can't</u> hunt foxes.
 b. We <u>won't</u> be going to the show.
 c. <u>Haven't</u> you seen that movie?
 d. The lawn <u>hasn't</u> been moved.

4. Answers will vary.

Student Page 32 (page 68)

1. a. The tired cat d. Jill
 b. My best friend e. the bus
 c. a large shopping center

2. a. The <u>snakes slide</u> into the hollow log.
 b. <u>The passengers are</u> boarding the jet plane.
 c. The <u>girls are</u> in the tree house.
 d. <u>The</u> golden <u>leaves were</u> falling to the ground.
 e. In the night sky, the <u>stars are</u> twinkling.

Student Page 33 (page 69)

1. I'll – I will, he's – he is, they've – they have, we're – we are, she'd – she would, you've – you have; I'm – I am, you're – you are, they're – they are, it's – it is, he'll – he will, we've – we have; I've – I have, you'll – you will, he'd – he would, she's – she is, they'd – they would, we'll – we will

2. a. they've, they have
 b. It's, It is
 c. I'm, I am; she'll, she will
 d. We're, We are; you've, you have
 e. I'd, I would; they're, they are
 f. You'll, You will; he's, he is

3. a. You're c. They're
 b. We're   d. its

Student Page 34 (page 70)

1. Answers will vary.

2. a. is
 b. are
 c. are
 Drawings will vary.

3. Sentences will vary; past tense (all)

Student Page 35 (page 71)

1. Answers will vary.

2. a. helped i. lived
 b. rained j. invited
 c. cooked k. planned
 d. stayed l. stepped
 e. wanted m. pinned
 f. shared n. robbed
 g. closed o. grinned
 h. changed

3. a. ate g. grew
 b. gave h. did
 c. came i. ran
 d. dug j. had
 e. was k. stood
 f. sang l. broke

4. a. bought d. sat
 b. lit   e. saw
 c. ran   f. spent

Student Page 36 (page 72)

1. Answers will vary.

2. Drawings will vary.

3. a. past f. future
 b. present g. past
 c. future h. present
 d. future i. present
 e. past

Student Page 37 (page 73)

1. walking, prided, feeling, looking, hopped, snatched, frightened, going, asked, trying

2. Answers will vary.

3.

Student Page 38 (page 74)

1. a. to make smaller
 b. to say you're sorry
 c. to make use of
 d. to find fault with
 e. to remember something seen before

2. Answers will vary.

3. a. terrify d. beautify
 b. signify e. identify
 c. notify

4. a. investigate d. nominate
 b. operate   e. irrigate
 c. excavate

Assessment—Verbs (pages 75 and 76)

1. was, had tricked, decided, would pay, mixed, shaped, put, will catch, thought, laughed

2. a. will return; future (green)
 b. Add; present (blue)
 c. waited; past (red)
 d. is harvesting; present (blue)
 e. will watch; future (green)
 f. were damaged; past (red)
 g. are playing; present (blue)
 h. drove; past (red)
 i. will enter; future (green)
 j. polished; past (red)

3. a. v   d. v, n, v
 b. v, n e. n, n
 c. n, v

4. Answers will vary.

5. a. couldn't d. Can't
 b. They're e. You're
 c. he'd

6. a. flies   d. lives
   b. shines   e. are
   c. rides

7. riding, buying, wanted, asked, floated

ADVERBS

Student Page 39 (page 80)

1. a. how   d. when
   b. when   e. where
   c. where

2. a. loudly   d. there
   b. early   e. now, later
   c. quietly   f. softly

3. Answers will vary.

Student Page 40 (page 81)

1. a. away, WH   d. often, W
   b. around, WH   e. noisily, H
   c. easily, H   f. daily, W

2. Possible answers:
   a. quietly/quickly   d. Wearily
   b. Yesterday   e. backwards
   c. here/there   f. often/sometimes

3. a. called, how   d. sit, where; work, how
   b. watch, when   e. galloped, where
   c. tied, how

4. a. carefully   c. clearly
   b. patiently   d. kindly

Student Page 41 (page 82)

1. a. dangerously   d. gently
   b. heavily   e. proudly
   c. Silently

2. a. badly   d. kindly
   b. Carefully   e. quietly
   c. noisily

3. a. He crept silently up the stairs.
   b. I spoke clearly, so everyone could hear.
   c. He knocked loudly, and the door opened.
   d. Jeff ran slowly and lost the race.
   e. It rained heavily for many days.
   f. She waited patiently at the bus stop.

Student Page 42 (page 83)

1. a. safely   d. kindly
   b. softly/quietly   e. early
   c. always   f. later

2.
```
Y L T F O S J O K R
L B G E L D W X L B
H I G H P R Q I H D
G A N V O A U V E L
U B A C K W A R D S
O E Z E L P E F I O
R L G H Q U T M S U
D O S L O W L Y T T
R W Y L T E I U Q H
```

3. Answers will vary.

Student Page 43 (page 84)

1. a. Where   d. When
   b. Why   e. Why
   c. How   f. How

2. Answers will vary.

3. a. Why are the children laughing?
   b. When is the final football game?
   c. How do you make a paper plane?
   d. Where can I buy a comic book?

Assessment—Adverbs (pages 85 and 86)

1. a. how   d. when
   b. when   e. where
   c. how   f. how

2. once, quickly, excitedly, anxiously, impatiently, always, late, crossly, properly, loudly

3. a. lazily   e. busily
   b. steeply   f. strongly
   c. wildly   g. thickly
   d. tidily   h. roughly

4. Answers will vary.

5. a. turn   d. is strolling
   b. make   e. is raining
   c. turned

6. a. late   d. smoothly
   b. always   e. quickly
   c. outside   f. carelessly

7. a. fairly   d. busy
   b. wisely   e. quiet
   c. slowly

8. a. Come outside and play with me.
   b. She fell heavily and hurt her knee.
   c. The horse galloped away across the sandy hill.
   d. The truck bumped noisily over the rough road.
   e. The sun shone brightly in the blue sky.

PREFIXES

Student Page 44 (page 87)

1. a. disappeared   e. undecided
   b. untrue   f. disagree
   c. impatient   g. inappropriate
   d. inaccurate   h. impossible

2. a. upstairs, downstairs
   b. upstream, downstream
   c. uphill, downhill
   d. upright, downright
   e. upgrade, downgrade
   f. overweight, underweight
   g. overtake, undertake
   h. overrate, underrate
   i. overestimate, underestimate
   j. oversized, undersized

Student Page 45 (page 88)

1. a. discovered   d. underway
   b. informed   e. converted
   c. rectangle   f. reconnected

2. a. afternoon   d. predict
   b. prepackaged   e. aftershocks
   c. prehistoric   f. aftershave

PREPOSITIONS & PHRASES

Student Page 46 (page 92)

1. a. We all laughed at the clown.
   b. I only took one apple from the bowl.
   c. She has been waiting for you.
   d. He shared the chocolate with me.
   e. The tired farmer sat under a tree.

2. Check drawings.

3. a. under the rocking chair
   b. At home
   c. on the wall
   d. down the street
   e. in the sky
   f. in the garage
   g. around the lake

Student Page 47 (page 93)
Answers will vary.

Student Page 48 (page 94)

1. a. cups   d. box
   b. chocolate   e. bell
   c. man

2. a. the curtains over the window
   b. the vase on the table
   c. the dog with the flea collar

ANSWER KEY

d. the water in the jug
e. the cat under the bed

3. Answers will vary.

Student Page 49 (page 95)

1. a. when   d. why
   b. where   e. when
   c. how   f. why

2. a. He polished his shoes with a soft cloth.
   b. The train will depart in ten minutes.
   c. Below the waves dived the spear fisherman.
   d. Take another apple for your sister.
   e. During the storm, branches broke like matchsticks.

3. Answers will vary.

Assessment—Prepositions & Phrases (pages 96–98)

1. On Saturday morning; to the beach; for the day; in a park; In the afternoon; in the surf; of mini golf; in the tide pools with Mom; in the late afternoon; into bed

2. Check drawings.

3. Answers will vary.

4. a. where   c. how, where
   b. when, where   d. why

5. a. girl   d. everyone
   b. cup   e. people
   c. child

6. a. The cowboy rode with great skill at the rodeo.
   b. I borrowed a book about China from the library.
   c. The dog waited by the kitchen door for a bone.
   d. We all cheered for the team who came first.
   e. Skating at the ice rink is such fun.

7. a. She whistled for her dog.
   b. Before winter, the farmer will plant his crop.
   c. The firefighter called out in a loud voice.
   d. In the backyard, you'll see our tree house.
   e. Don't go without a hat.

8. a. The plane flew (over/above) the city.
   b. He went (down) the ladder.
   c. Place a chair (under) the table.
   d. We played a game (without/against) Ravi.
   e. Let's go jogging (beside, by, past, near) the lake.

9. a. which   d. where
   b. where   e. which
   c. which

SENTENCES

Student Page 50 (page 102)

1. b, d, f, g, i, j

2. My sister and I went walking in the park. **We** saw a boy walking his dog and a girl on a red scooter. **My** sister wanted an ice cream. **We** found a stand and bought two big cones. **We** sat under a big tree to eat them.

3. Answers will vary.

Student Page 51 (page 103)

1. Check statements.

2. a. fact   d. opinion
   b. opinion   e. opinion
   c. fact

3. Answers will vary.

Student Page 52 (page 104)

1. Suggested answers:
   a. The family is reading a book.
   b. There are four people on the bed.
   c. A man is helping the children.
   d. The boy is playing at the beach.
   e. The boy is building a sand castle.
   f. It is summer.

2. a. A spider has eight legs.
   b. An oasis is found in the desert.
   c. You would go to the theater to see a play or movie.
   d. A doctor or nurse helps sick people.
   e. My favorite snack is . . .
   f. A rainbow appears when the sun comes out after rain.

Student Page 53 (page 105)

1. a. I went to the pet shop to buy a white rabbit.
   b. The wallet was left on the bus.
   c. Man overboard!
   d. Let's play baseball in the backyard.
   e. What a wonderful party!

2. Answers will vary.

3. Check drawings.

Student Page 54 (page 106)

1. a. Wear
   b. Bake
   c. Write
   d. Stand
   e. Pass
   f. Bend
   The verbs are all at the beginning of the sentence.

2. Answers will vary.

Student Page 55 (page 107)

1. a. The hot air balloon
   b. A camel train
   c. the go-cart
   d. My aunt
   e. tomato juice
   f. Golden autumn leaves

2. a. My red bike   d. All the students
   b. my little sister   e. the police car
   c. A baby panda   f. Your baseball cap

Student Page 56 (page 108)
Answers will vary.

Student Page 57 (page 109)

1. a. so   d. and
   b. but   e. so
   c. but

2. Answers will vary.

3. a. Tom wants to go in the pool, but he can't swim.
   b. Mia has black hair, but Jacqui is blonde.
   c. The bell has rung, so you may go home.
   d. Greg knocked on the door, but no one answered.
   e. I like coffee, and I also like tea.
   f. It rained heavily, so the pool is full.

Student Page 58 (page 111)

1. a. Kyle was unhappy
   b. a car came rushing around the corner
   c. we will go to the skateboard park
   d. I collected a bucket of shells
   e. The audience went home

2. a. where she was going
   b. because we didn't win our last game
   c. until I tell you to move
   d. Although he is small
   e. before the sun goes down

3. Answers will vary.

Student Page 59 (page 112)

1. Answers will vary.

2. a. who   d. that
   b. which   e. which
   c. that   f. who

Student Page 60 (page 113)

1. a. when   f. where
   b. where   g. why
   c. when   h. why
   d. why   i. when
   e. when   j. when

2.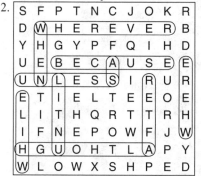

Student Page 61 (page 114)

1. a. until everyone was quiet
   b. When I broke my leg
   c. unless you wear a hat
   d. before you speak
   e. then to the pool
   f. because I was too young
   g. Whenever you can come
   h. while you get your backpack

2. a. while   d. where
   b. When   e. Although
   c. because

Student Page 62 (page 115)

1. a. horse   d. people
   b. Everyone   e. meat
   c. necklace

2. a. who   d. who
   b. which   e. that
   c. that

3. Answers will vary.

Student Page 63 (page 116)

1. "Dad's taking us across the town by train this holiday," said Jessica excitedly. "Where are you going, Eddie?"

   "We're going to stay in a hotel, just south of Sydney," Eddie replied. "We'll be right beside the beach."

   "That sounds like fun, too," said Jessica. "We should get some great photos."

   "Yeah. Mom has just bought a digital camera, and she wants to try it out," said Eddie. Then he smiled, "She's not very good with techno things, though."

2. a. "Please come to the movies with me,"
   b. "Who has been sleeping in my bed?"
   c. "Let me show you the menu,"
   d. "We'll need to score an early goal,"
   e. "Just stir in the flour slowly,"

Student Page 64 (page 117)

1. a. "What game do you want to play?" asked Jeremy.
      "Why don't we have a game of marbles?" answered Karl.
   b. Michael called out, "Has anyone seen my football?"
      "No, Michael!" shouted everyone altogether.
   c. "Where is the nearest shop?" asked the man from Africa.
      "Do you want me to take you?" asked Jack.

2. Answers will vary.

3. "How was your first day back to school?" Aunt Jean asked.

   "It was great," said Sally. "My teacher's name is Ms. Fiz, and I sat beside my best friend!"

   "What was the best thing you did today?" Aunt Jean asked.

   Sally said, "The teacher took photos of all the children. She told us that we would be writing a little bit about ourselves to go in a class book."

   "That sounds interesting," said Aunt Jean.

Assessment—Sentences (pages 118–120)

1. b, e

2. a. fact   d. opinion
   b. opinion   e. fact
   c. fact

3. Answers will vary.

4. a. Play   d. Slice
   b. Cut   e. Toss
   c. Wash

5. a. The circus clown
   b. muddy, brown water
   c. the sound of rumbling thunder
   d. the car
   e. a tawny, gray owl

6. a. and   d. and
   b. but   e. but
   c. so

7. a. The twins were very excited when they opened their presents.
   b. This is the grandfather clock that was in my uncle's house.
   c. Because his ankle was sore, he could not join in the game.
   d. There is the man who was elected senator.
   e. Until it rained, there was no water in the tank.

8. Answers will vary.

9. a. who   c. which
   b. that

10. "Why are you boys so late coming back to class?" the teacher asked.

    Ben replied, "We were in the library and didn't hear the bell."

11. Mozart was a talented musician. He was born in Austria two hundred and fifty years ago. He was a clever little boy. Mozart soon learned to play the piano. He wrote many wonderful pieces of music.

    Many people believe Mozart to be the greatest composer who has ever lived. I would agree with them.

WORDWORKS CARDS (pages 125–129)

1. buttered bread, protected animal, washing machine, scented flowers, fading colors, caring person, dancing shoes, unfinished work, training run, garbled message

ANSWER KEY

2. lost/found, fresh/stale, smooth/rough, late/early, tall/short, old/young, blunt/sharp, green/ripe, high/low, east/west

3. tennis = game played with racquets; caravan = a group of vehicles; laces = strings to tie up shoes; bonnet = hat tied under the chin; tripod = three-legged camera stand; pumpkin = vegetable grown on a vine; panther = black, wild animal; parcel = a package; cello = stringed instrument; court = place to play tennis

4. firewood, homework, horseback, waterfall, driveway, bedside, basketball, popcorn, snowstorm, cornflakes

5. slithering snake, crunchy apple, humorous story, sharp sword, autumn leaves, dangerous animal, heavy rainfall, elderly person, sour lemons, joyful celebration

6. Nouns = napkin, court, knuckle, flavor, doorbell, bundle, chore, tower, youth

   Adjectives = lazy, active, sensible, magical, curious, handsome, enchanted, famous, robust

   Adjective or Noun = dependent, mystery

7. Nouns = riddle, trouble, jungle, kettle, pimple

   Verbs = settle, meddle, fumble, mangle

   Noun or Verb = rattle

8. Dad's car, teachers' books, bus' window, horses' bridles, children's coats, dogs' collars, clown's act, day's end

9. frosty, runny, tasty, spotty, lumpy, slimy, handy, snappy, rosy, gritty, fishy, misty

10. noisily, happily, gladly, merrily, swiftly, widely, quickly, feebly, lazily, promptly, flatly, lightly

11. did, jumped, had, found, raced, cried, hopped, stayed, was, fell, sat, changed

12. hopping, facing, drying, flowing, sitting, depending, stumbling, crushing, roaring, admitting, confiding, skiing

13. Nouns = angel, tale, pie, statue, flesh, jungle, violin, prince, basin

    Verbs = prance, sharpen, juggle, fail, melt, graze, gallop, spill

    Noun or Verb = grind, pickle, swelter

14. Answers will vary.

15. Answers will vary.

16. He, It, It, her, her, It, I, I, it, she

17. Answers will vary.

18. roads, peaches, ladies, bones, bodies, teeth, potatoes, leaves, monkeys, geese

19. Answers will vary.

20. coach, deer, He, boys, I, Kate and Sue, cans, gymnasts, Max, snake

21. Male = gander, stallion, rooster, husband, nephew; Female = cow, doe, niece, mare, aunt; Either = partner, cousin, adult, gymnast, pilot; Neither = cabbage, cyclone, mountain, shack, computer

22. can't = cannot, hasn't = has not, I've = I have, we'll = we will, they'd = they would, we're = we are, you've = you have, she'd = she would or she had, he's = he is, they've = they have, you'll = you will, we'd = we would or we had, it's = it is, won't = will not, she's = she is or she has, he'll = he will

23. Saying = murmured, giggled, stammered, mentioned, sighed, tittered, scoffed, commented; Doing = sprinted, stumbled, clambered, wandered, lazed, sailed, feasted, sheltered

24. Definitions will vary.

25. Animal = chimpanzee, panda, otter, zebra, donkey; Person = athlete, comedian, pilot, usher, ranger; Place = beach, theater, Italy, kitchen, stadium; Thing = shovel, fence, scissors, ladder, lantern

26. tame/wild, ugly/beautiful, honest/dishonest, tidy/untidy, fast/slow, busy/idle, straight/crooked, long/short, wide/narrow, proud/ashamed

27. Answers will vary.

28. cannot or can, does or did, was, have, will, has, was, Did or Have, Will, Have

29. Person = calm, athletic, young, kind, clever, curious; Place = rocky, calm, deserted, shady, sandy, crowded, restful; Thing = rocky, broken, chewy, sparkling, crumpled, plastic, shiny

30. She will = She'll, I have = I've, He is = He's, They would = They'd, You are = You're, We have = We've, I would = I'd, They are = They're, She would = She'd, I am = I'm, It is = It's, He will = He'll, You have = You've, We are = We're

FACT FINDERS CARDS (pages 170–184)

1. history, hibernate, profession

2. glimmer, congratulate, knuckle

3. orchard, label, shrub, mirror

4. cinnamon, massive, venom

5. gravel, massage, publish, wan

6. clamber, starboard, warp

7. wilt, khaki, rancid

8. blacktop, Buzzard, Feral

9. original, curb, whistle

10. leader, draft, comedy

11. venue, tidbit, stampede

12. severe, portrait, forage

13. thorn, mimic, ignore, cymbals

14. Bulldozer, ponder, carnival

15. gully, brochure

16. arena, Lava, blurb

17. employee, gradual, lazy

18. navigate, Vandal, promptly

19. broad, veil, lagoon

20. cancel, nimble, Peppercorn

21. mast, hood, bacteria

22. hamper, turkey, charcoal

23. assortment, estimate, rare

24. penniless, paperback, landscape

25. pendulum, famine, squid

26. orphan, Hemisphere, enormous

27. hazel, knowledge, flounce

28. diploma, solar, calico

29. spine, decade, glacier, pain

30. hacienda, haggle

GRAMMAR TASK CARDS

(pages 185–198)

Nouns 1

1. Sentences should be written for cow, rope, elephant, cart, and seaweed.

2. a. my cat's paws or my cats' paws
   b. Ashar's bike
   c. the foxes' tails
   d. the cup's handle
   e. the students' classroom or the student's classroom
   f. some birds' feathers
   g. the cooks' saucepans or the cook's saucepans
   h. a bee's wings
   i. a teacher's meeting
   j. the snake's skin

3. a. a flock of sheep
   b. a mob of kangaroos
   c. a school of fish
   d. a litter of pups
   e. a fleet of ships
   f. a pod of whales
   g. a clutch of eggs
   h. a band of robbers
   i. a pack of dogs
   j. a bunch of roses

Nouns 2

1. Places: prison, school, cornfield, waterhole, church; Things: clouds, kettle, tulips, feather, towel

2. Shahil, India, Simran, December, Christmas Day, Stanford University, Shahil, New York Yankees

3. Answers will vary (e.g., a. apple; b. staircase; c. mobile; d. motorcycle).

Nouns 3

1. a. sender
   b. goodness
   c. movement
   d. goalkeeper
   e. rider
   f. statement
   g. kindness, kinder
   h. exporter
   i. management
   j. richer/richness

2. Answers will vary (e.g., a. ball; b. puppy; c. road; d. brick; e. brass band).

Nouns 4

1. a. the
   b. a
   c. an
   d. the
   e. an
   f. The

2. Answers will vary—grandfather, lifetime, nighttime, nightstand, headpiece, headdress, overdress, overhead, overweight, underweight, understand, underline, timeline, headlight, timepiece, lightweight, headline.

Adjectives 1

1. Answers will vary.

2. Answers will vary.

Adjectives 2

1. painted fence, growing plants, chewing gum, ploughed field, gaping hole, bundled sticks

2. People: talented, wealthy, thoughtful, upset, friendly, lonely, careless; Things: unusual, long, crumpled, metal, heated, expensive, sharp

3. Sentences should be written for dangerous, salty, famous, happy, golden

Adjectives 3

1. two, old, iron, rusty, heavy, rough, overgrown, old, crumbling, sandstone, two, falling, twisted, large, wooden, broken, thick, scared

2. a. comfortable
   b. restful/restless
   c. likeable
   d. useful/useless
   e. helpful/helpless
   f. tireless
   g. reasonable
   h. forceful
   i. effortless
   j. workable

Adjectives 4

1. Answers will vary.

2. b. longer, longest
   c. bright, brighter
   d. dirtier, dirtiest
   e. steeper, steepest
   f. wide, widest
   g. happy, happier
   h. good, better, best

3. happy/sad, old/new or young, stale/fresh, fast/slow, long/short, narrow/wide, straight/crooked, sour/sweet, light/dark or heavy, kind/unkind, clean/dirty, strong/weak, small/large, low/high

Pronouns 1

1. a. her, her
   b. She
   c. hers, her
   d. Hers
   e. She, her

2. a. their
   b. there
   c. there
   d. their, their
   e. there, their

Pronouns 2

(Sample Answers)

1. a. Jack left his bag on the bus.
   b. The boys put all their toys away in their toy box.
   c. Did you see the zebras at the zoo?
   d. Wait for me and we can go together.
   e. "Give me back my ball, please," I said.

2. a. Who
   b. Which
   c. What
   d. Which
   e. Whose

Pronouns 3

1. a. its
   b. my/my
   c. your/my/his/her
   d. mine/his/hers/yours
   e. his/her/my/your
   f. ours/yours/theirs/mine

2. a. my
   b. them
   c. us, you
   d. his, me
   e. my, his
   f. They
   g. me

Pronouns 4

1. Answers will vary.

2. a. Jake
   b. Mom
   c. the class
   d. the painting
   e. Jen
   f. Ryan
   g. Ella and Jacob

Verbs 1

1. a. did
   b. done
   c. done
   d. Did
   e. did
   f. done
   g. done
   h. done
   Sentences will vary.

2. a. went
   b. gone
   c. gone
   d. went
   e. went
   f. gone
   g. went
   h. gone
   Sentences will vary.

Verbs 2

1. a. saw
   b. seen
   c. saw
   d. seen
   e. saw
   f. saw
   g. seen
   h. saw
   Sentences will vary.

2. throw, stir, listen, chew, choose, speak, has, seize, draw, construct

ANSWER KEY

Verbs 3

1. a. Sue and Lynn went for a walk on Sunday.
   b. The boys ate cashew nuts and drank lemonade.
   c. We thought his painting was the best one of all.
   d. They stood when the teacher came in.

2. a. didn't   g. won't
   b. couldn't   h. wasn't
   c. hasn't   i. aren't
   d. can't   j. haven't
   e. isn't   k. don't
   f. wouldn't   l. weren't

3. walking, whistled, walked, followed, walked, spotted, chased, barking, scurried, snapped, missed

Verbs 4

1. Answers will vary.

2. Doing: tumble, skip, wait, pinch, roll, ride; Saying: shout, roar, giggle, argue, scream, scold

3. a. she'll   g. they're
   b. they've   h. he'd
   c. you're   i. she's
   d. he's   j. we'd
   e. we're   k. I'm
   f. I'd   l. we'll

Adverbs 1

1. Answers will vary.

2. a. recklessly, down   d. down
   b. together, quietly   e. backwards, over
   c. yesterday

Adverbs 2

1. a. loudly   f. never
   b. after   g. quickly/fast
   c. downwards   h. backwards
   d. early   i. up
   e. outside   j. north

2. a. dangerously   f. lazily
   b. stonily   g. famously
   c. grandly   h. doubtfully
   d. seriously   i. stupidly
   e. widely   j. happily

3. a. Where/When/How/Why
   b. Why
   c. How
   d. When/Why/How
   e. How/When/Where/Why

Adverbs 3

1. a. heavily   d. kindly
   b. slowly   e. foolishly
   c. softly

2. Answers will vary.

3. a. when   d. when
   b. how   e. how
   c. where

Adverbs 4

1. a. crept   d. go, come
   b. landed   e. buy
   c. laughed

2. a. sadly   g. loosely
   b. inside   h. painlessly
   c. clumsily   i. heavily
   d. slowly   j. unkindly
   e. coldly   k. neatly
   f. below   l. after

Phrases 1

1. Drawings will vary.

2. Answers will vary.

Phrases 2

1. a. under the bed   d. behind the shed
   b. After dinner   e. in that bag
   c. during the night

2. a. lighthouse   d. path
   b. animal   e. shirt
   c. leaves

Phrases 3

1. Answers will vary.

2. a. where   d. why
   b. how   e. when
   c. how

Prepositions 1

1. Answers will vary.

2. a. in   d. with
   b. of   e. At, for
   c. on, of

Sentences 1

1. a. Cats stalk birds.
   c. The man stroked his beard.
   f. We sang around the piano.
   g. Wild horses galloped by the farm.
   i. They go camping by the lake.
   j. Was there someone at the door?

2. Sentences will vary.

3. Answers will vary.

Sentences 2

1. Answers will vary.

2. Drawings will vary.

Sentences 3

1. a. Jayne likes pears, but Con likes plums.
   b. It is late, so I must leave.
   c. I ate a cookie, and I drank a glass of milk.
   d. The lightning flashed, and the thunder crashed.
   e. I would come with you, but I don't have time.
   f. He shouted loudly, but no one heard him.

2. a. The boys in the go-kart rushed down the hill.
   b. My yellow kite hit the top of the tree.
   c. After dinner, Mandy and I played chess.
   d. A large black spider dangled in its web.
   e. A tiny village was nestled at the foot of the mountain.

Sentences 4

1. Answers will vary.

2. a. cyclones
   b. all students
   c. the top-ranked tennis player
   d. all homework
   e. you

3. "Can I help you, sir?" asked the salesman.

   "Yes, please," said Mr. Dobbs. "I would like some rechargeable batteries."

   "Of course, sir," said the salesman. "What size do you need?"